W9-DHK-391

THE
ITALIAN IN AMERICA

Visit of the American Bankers' Association at the Italian-Swiss Colony, Asti, Sonoma Co., California. Pompeian Villa of Cav. A. Sbarboro

THE
ITALIAN IN AMERICA

BY

ELIOT LORD

JOHN J. D. TRENOR

SAMUEL J. BARROWS

 BOOKS FOR LIBRARIES PRESS
FREEPORT, NEW YORK

First Published 1905

Reprinted 1970

104607

INTERNATIONAL STANDARD BOOK NUMBER:

0-8369-5530-7

LIBRARY OF CONGRESS CATALOG CARD NUMBER:

71-130557

PRINTED IN THE UNITED STATES OF AMERICA

PREFACE.

The design of " The Italian in America " is to present clearly the contribution of Italy to American development and citizenship. The work is one of a series reviewing the influx of the various racial strains and nationalities that are making up the composite American. The authors have in view simply the recital of facts for impartial consideration, for no concern of this country is more momentous and urgent than the national dealing with the problems of immigration, congestion, distribution and education for American standards of living and citizenship. To exclude what is essentially bad or unfusible from any source—to welcome and utilize what is essentially good and helpful, even if yet imperfectly developed, is in the judgment of the authors the true American policy.

CONTENTS

CHAPTER I

The Flow of Emigration

CHAPTER II

The Inheritance and Progress of United Italy

CHAPTER III

The Causes and Regulation of Italian Emigration

Contents

CHAPTER IV

Italian Settlement in American Cities

CHAPTER V

In Competition and Association

Contents

CHAPTER VI

In the Mining Fields

CHAPTER VII

On Farm and Plantation

CHAPTER VIII

Rising Demand for Italian Immigrant Labor

Contents

CHAPTER IX

The Call for Better Distribution

CHAPTER X

Pauperism, Disease and Crime

Contents

CHAPTER XI

Progressive Education and Assimilation

CHAPTER XII

Privileges and Duties of Italian-American Citizenship

Contents

THE ITALIAN IN AMERICA

CHAPTER I

It is only of late years that any study of Italian immigration, capacity and character has become of any national concern to this country. Long ago there used to be a childish patter in our primary schools: "In 1492 Columbus crossed the ocean blue." Most of the children had in mind that Columbus was born in Italy, and in the upper schools there was some slight tracing of the opening of North America to immigrants through the guidance of the Cabots and Verrazano. But there was little reckoning of any contribution of living Italians to American development. Our scholars, at large, were far more attracted by the memorials of the Old Roman Empire than by the present day problems of Italy. The uncovering of a headless and armless bust was much more interesting than the inspection of an Italian rookery.

We knew in a general way the dreary annals of Italian decadence—of the provincial and civic alienations—of the

1

regal and oligarchic impositions—of foreign invasions and internecine conflicts —of the greedy extortions of the ruling classes and the heavy burdens of the toiling masses. We were moved to sympathy with the ardor and struggles of high spirited patriots for the redemption of their fatherland.   Garibaldi, Cavour, Mazzini—all who shared in the labors and perils through which Italy was freed and unified—were honored in America perhaps more highly than in any other country in the world, outside of their native land.

But we had no thought of any particular appeal of Italy to us or of her entry in force into the pressing problems of our own life and growth.   Outside of the passing survey of tourists, the Italian common people were practically known to us only by the sight of a rambling organ-grinder or image-seller.   This travesty of the wandering minstrel of romance, twitching his plaintive monkey, and this peddler of plaster casts on a headboard, were the current expositions of Italy in this country for many years, until the common people began to come over in swarms and enlarge our familiar view of the·Italian in America.

There is a notable peculiarity in the flow of Italian immigration to this country.   From the earliest days of the colonization of America up to less than a generation ago, the influx from Italy was barely a trickle, so inconsiderable that a microscope is almost needed to distinguish the Italian resident population in 1850 as portrayed

The Flow of Emigration

in the Census plate (No. 17) showing the proportion and advance of leading foreign born nationalities in the closing half of the last century. Only a slight advance in numbers is shown in the plates for the succeeding censuses of 1860 and 1870, though the exact amount of the Italian influx during these decades is not strictly determinable from the lack of reliable records.

In 1880 an appreciable increase appears, but the advance was even then of comparatively inconsiderable importance. Though it was more than tripled in the succeeding decade from 1880 to 1890, the Italian population in the United States by the record of the census of 1890 is given as only 182,580. The total influx up to this date can scarcely have exceeded 500,000, and the greater part of this total was composed of those making only a transient stay. This is plainly determined by the statistics reported by Dr. J. H. Senner, formerly United States Commissioner of Immigration, computing the total number of immigrants from Italy between the years 1872 and 1890 as 356,062. With any just allowance for settlement by Italians prior to 1872, it is obvious that more than half of the immigrants within the recorded period had left the United States for their own or other countries, although a progressive increase in the percentage of settlers is noted with probable certainty.

The record of immigration for 1890 and subsequent years to date is more exactly traceable.

The Italian in America

IMMIGRATION FROM ITALY TO THE UNITED STATES

	1890	1891	1892	1893
Italy—Continental	51,799	72,704	59,160	71,145
Sicily and Sardinia	294	3,351	2,977	1,771

	1894	1895	1896	1897	1898
Italy	43,967	36,961	68,060	59,431	58,613

	1899	1900	1901	1902	1903	1904
Italy	77,419	100,135	135,996	178,375	230,622	193,296

This gives a total, from the census year of 1890 up to and including the census year of 1900, of 655,888, but this influx only increased the number of resident Italians, according to the last census, to a total of 484,703 in the United States, including all insular territories.

The aggregate increase of the influx in the four years succeeding the census year of 1890 mounted up to 738,289, but this, as above, does not represent the actual increase of resident population born in Italy, for this total is diminished by the numbers returning annually, as well as by deaths, so that no correct estimate of the existing addition to our population through immigration from Italy is likely to exceed materially one per cent. of the present population of this country. This exhibit compiled from official returns suffices to mark the futility of the assumption that the influx from Italy is affecting to any material extent the dominant racial character of our population.

How this influx was distributed up to the close of the census year 1900 is officially determined in the record of

The Flow of Emigration

the last census, marking the apportionment in five comprehensive divisions, and the individual states as follows:

	1900 Population born in Italy.
The United States	484,207
North Atlantic Division	352,065
Maine	1,334
New Hampshire	947
Vermont	2,154
Massachusetts	28,785
Rhode Island	8,972
Connecticut	19,105
New York	182,248
New Jersey	41,865
Pennsylvania	66,655
South Atlantic Division	10,509
Delaware	1,122
Maryland	2,449
District of Columbia	930
Virginia	781
West Virginia	2,921
North Carolina	201
South Carolina	180
Georgia	218
Florida	1,707
North Central Division	55,085
Ohio	11,321
Indiana	1,327
Illinois	23,523
Michigan	6,178
Wisconsin	2,172

	1900. Population born in Italy.
Minnesota	2,222
Iowa	1,198
Missouri	4,345
North Dakota	700
South Dakota	360
Nebraska	752
Kansas	987
South Central Division	**26,158**
Kentucky	679
Tennessee	1,222
Alabama	862
Mississippi	845
Louisiana	17,431
Texas	3,942
Indian Territory	573
Oklahoma	28
Arkansas	576
Western Division	**40,210**
Montana	2,199
Wyoming	781
Colorado	6,818
New Mexico	661
Arizona	699
Utah	1,062
Nevada	1,296
Idaho	779
Washington	2,124
Oregon	1,014
California	22,777

From this table a regrettable lack of a better proportioned distribution of the influx thus far is evident. 72.7

per cent. of the Italians in this country are clustered in the North Atlantic Division, and 11.4 per cent. in the North Central Division. There is a better average distribution in the Western Division, containing 8.3 per cent. of the Italian population, though by far the greater part are settled in California and Colorado. In the South Central Division there are 5.4 per cent., Louisiana and Texas containing by far the greater proportion of this percentage. The South Atlantic Division has thus far attracted less than a thirtieth part of the number in the North Atlantic Division, and a little more than a fiftieth part of the total of Italians in this country, showing a percentage of only 2.2.

It is interesting to mark also that the relative contribution of Italy to the total foreign born population of this country was less than a twentieth at the last census taking, or in exact percentage, 4.7. Although the number of Italians in the South Central Division was less than a twelfth of the number in the North Atlantic Division, it is noteworthy that the comparative percentage in the former, 7.3, was almost exactly as great as the percentage in the latter division, 7.4.

The tendency of the influx to cluster in cities, the more or less congested centres of population, is pronounced, and will be particularly accounted for. Of the total population born in Italy, in this country—302,324, constituting 62.4 per cent., were resident in the 160 principal

7

cities in 1900. This is considerably less than the percentage of the Russian born population in the same cities,
74.9, with the exception of the natives of Russian-Poland,
showing only a percentage of 62.7; but it is considerably
more than the average of the total foreign born, 49.5.
It is worth remarking, however, that the percentage of
Italians attracted to the cities is almost exactly the same
as that of the Irish, 62. per cent. of whom are recorded
as residing in these 160 principal cities. In view of the
relatively long residence of the Irish in this country, the
attraction to the city, so far as it is objectionable, is apparently more lamentable than in the case of the Italians,
though they are far more rarely reproached for the aggravation of congestion.

In twenty-six of the cities noted, the Italian born population exceeded 1,000, the numerical distribution being
in order:

1.	New York	145,433
2.	Philadelphia	17,830
3.	Chicago	16,008
4.	Boston	13,738
5.	Newark	8,537
6.	Providence	6,256
7.	New Orleans	5,866
8.	Pittsburg	5,709
9.	Buffalo	5,669
10.	New Haven	5,262
11.	Paterson	4,266
12.	Jersey City	3,832
13.	Cleveland	3,065

The Flow of Emigration

14.	Hoboken	2,360
15.	St. Louis	2,227
16.	Baltimore	2,042
17.	Waterbury	2,007
18.	Hartford	1,952
19.	Utica	1,661
20.	Bridgeport	1,436
21.	Trenton	1,337
22.	Youngstown	1,331
23.	Scranton	1,312
24.	Rochester	1,278
25.	Syracuse	1,232
26.	Kansas City	1,034

Since the date of the census record it is certain that the Italian born population in all American cities has increased more or less through the influx of immigration, for they have received, as before, the greater part of those coming over, but the distribution has varied widely in some cases, changing materially the order given in the city record of 1900, and including cities not before mentioned, like Schenectady and Los Angeles, in the stated list.

In the computation of the Italian population in America it is usual to include the first generation, at least, born here, having one or both parents born in Italy. This enumeration raises the total of the so-called Italian population in America, according to the statistical tables prepared under the direction of the Italian Chamber of Commerce, to 748,855 in the year 1900. This number will be slightly reduced if the reckoning is confined to those having an Italian father, in which case the total

9

is computed to be 742,197. According to this latter computation, the percentage of Italians residing in American cities is 77.9, or more than three-fourths of the total.

The same statistical tables give the Italian population of the State of New York, including children whose fathers were born in Italy, as 272,572 in 1900. The city of New York in that year contained more than two-fifths of the total in the State, or in exact figures, 225,026. The rapid increase in the State during the last three years is doubtlessly quite accurately marked in the March (1904) Bulletin of the Italian Chamber of Commerce. It is here computed that there were in Greater New York at the end of the year 1903, 382,775 Italians, including children whose fathers were born in Italy, and that the number in the entire State had risen to 486,175.

The division of sexes in the total of Italian immigration has not been exactly marked, though it is reckoned that the proportion of males to females has been at least four to one, and probably not less than five to one. For the past decade, however, it has been repeatedly noted that the percentage of women among these immigrants has been increasing, indicating a progressive firmness of settlement here and a rising intention to reside here permanently. This tendency was first particularly marked by Dr. J. H. Senner, U. S. Commissioner of Immigration, in his discussion of "Immigration from Italy" in the

The Flow of Emigration

North American Review for June, 1896. He observed that the percentage of women and children in the annual Italian immigration to this country was even then steadily rising. This was accompanied by a corresponding decrease in the "birds of passage," and the increasing tendency of Italian immigrants to definite settlement was proved, as he states, "by the systematic statistics kept at the Port of New York since July 1st, 1893, as to numbers of persons arriving to join members of their immediate families." Examination showed that from July 1st, 1893, to the end of December, 1895, more than one-third of the immigrants came to join members of their immediate families; and in this time the number of outgoing Italians exceeded the number of those who made their first entry into the United States by more than 25,000.

In the Report of the Industrial Commission on Immigration (1901, Vol. 15, p. 203), compiled from original figures in the annual reports of the Superintendent of Immigration, 1895–1899, the percentage of male immigrants from Northern Italy is given as 78.19, and the percentage of male immigrants from Southern Italy at 75.50. Subsequent reports of the Commissioner-General of Immigration show the percentage of male immigrants to be still declining, and in the latest annual report for the fiscal year ending June 30, 1904, of the total of 193,296 immigrants from Italy, including Sicily and Sardinia, 149,363 are entered as males and 43,933 as females, showing that more than one-fifth of the immigrants for this last year of record were women and girls. In the same report the number of Italian children under 14 years of age arriving during the same fiscal year is given as 24,528, showing a material increase in the settlement of families here.

It appears in the Report of the Commissioner-General of Immigration for the year ending June 30th, 1903, that of the 233,546 Italian immigrants arriving during that fiscal year at the ports of the United States and Canada, including those debarred, only 11,246 had reached the age of 45 years and over, and that 197,267 were between the ages of 14 and 45 years. The showing for this year of greatest influx to date is substantially typical, and apparently marks an extraordinary proportionate contribution of able-bodied persons to the working capital of this country. In view of the official returns, it is difficult to discern any foothold for the assumption of any reckless dumping of the aged and infirm or persons unable to work for their own support in the flow of immigration from Italy.

It was calculated with particular elaboration by Frederick Knapp, Commissioner of Immigration for the State of New York in 1870, that the average economic value of an able-bodied male immigrant over 20 years of age is $1,125. It is no practical concern whether this is an over or an under estimate. It is incontestable that every honest, able, willing laborer is a material addition to the working capital—the productive power of an undeveloped country. Unless it can be established by evidence that the mass of immigration from Italy is not composed of honest, able-bodied, willing laborers, there can be no economic warrant for any arbitrary resort to exclusion. If there are complaints of congestion, the rational economic resort is betterment of distribution—not the choking off of the productive flow.

An authoritative witness of the character and capacity of the bulk of the immigration from Italy, Adolfo Rossi, the present Supervisor of the Italian Emigration Department, has recently given evidence directly to the point in the weekly review of the New York Charity Organization Society *Charities*, published May 7th, 1904. It is his observation that emigration is taking away from his own country " the flower of our laboring class, which leaves Italy, not to seek a living, but greater comfort. To this, naturally, contributes the selection exercised by your immigration laws which let in only the good and reject the bad. My government allows the American commission of physicians of your own selection at Italian ports a pretty free hand. They examine the immigrant not only for trachoma, but make a fairly thorough examination for hernia, for diseases due to senility, etc., thus adding a potent artificial selection."

" Then I notice that the newspapers write of the influx

of a lot of poverty-stricken Italians. Just look at the facts: 84 per cent. of Italians coming here are between 18 and 45 years of age. That means that 84 per cent. of such immigrants belong to the working age. They are, in other words, producers. You get this product without the expense incurred in its raising. Every Italian of 18, for instance, costs his country, at the very lowest, $1,000 to bring him up. At 18 he begins to be a producer, but by leaving Italy the $1,000 invested by his country in him is lost. This 'human capital' of fresh, strong, young men is the contribution of Europe to the new land. We spend a thousand dollars to bring up and develop a young man, and then you reap the profits of the investment."

In face of the official reports and data here briefly summarized, there is a declared intention of influential formers of public opinion to urge legislation by Congress intentionally discriminating, in effect if not in form, against the flow of immigration from Italy in a way that will operate to exclude a great portion of it. In the Review of Special Reports in the Report of the Industrial Commission on Immigration to Congress, December 5th, 1901, the practical issue is assumedly brought to a head (p. LVIII) in the words: "The question now uppermost is that of the direct restriction of immigrants who are considered undesirable on general economic and social grounds, and not merely on the ground of contract labor." Unfortunately there is a lack of precision in the terms of this statement which opens it inevitably to further question. What is the standard of desirability which can or should be used in practice as a gauge for admission to this country, and who are to determine this standard?

There is, undoubtedly, a current opinion that the immigrants from Southern and Eastern Europe are relatively less desirable to this country than the immigrants as a body from Northern and Western Europe. This, indeed, has been so pronounced and outspoken that the present Commissioner-General of Immigration has apparently been led to set an official stamp of endorsement upon it in his report for the fiscal year ending June 30th, 1903 (p. 6).

" While some encouragement may be gained from consideration of the foregoing tabulated statements showing that the ratio of increase in immigration from Northern Europe was greatly in excess of that of the increase from Southern Europe, yet the fact remains that the great bulk of aliens added to our population during the year just passed came from Austria-Hungary, Italy and Russia, those three countries alone sending 572,726 of the total number of steerage aliens—more than two-thirds."

Nevertheless, it is scarcely credible that anyone will seriously propose that Congress should establish a geographical line of exclusion across the centre of Europe, cutting off immigration from Spain, Italy, Austria, South-

ern Russia and Greece. Nor is it probable that any avowed
discrimination will be proposed and enacted to the disadvantage of any particular nation or nations of Europe.
It is, however, much less certain that some covert discrimination will not be advanced by the pressure of prejudice in the form of a restrictive measure, ostensibly bearing
uniformly and equally on all nationalities contributing to
the stream of immigration. In fact, it is hardly disguised
that the proposed "educational test" for admission will
have this effect, as it has been expressly pointed out by
its advocates that it will bear most onerously on the nations
of Southern Europe, which their current opinion is disposed
to stamp as "undesirable."

Thus the issue will not be drawn barely whether it is
expedient or just to deny to an honest, willing laborer,
who is unable to read the Constitution of the United States,
permission to live and work for a livelihood in a republic
exalting the standard of liberty: but there will be reliance
on the fomented prejudice against the Southern Latin races
to urge this measure as a handy expedient of exclusion of
great part of the immigrants from Southern Europe, without seriously affecting the influx from Northern Europe,
which is now too strongly intrenched here for attack.

In view of this probability, it is of practical concern to
examine the grounds of this prejudice so far as it affects
the character and contribution of immigration from Italy,
which is the particular object of this special inquiry. A

Field of Sugar Cane, near Baxley, Georgia. Italian Cultivation

pithy, able and soberly phrased summary of the grounds of discrimination was made by Representative Samuel W. McCall of Massachusetts, who introduced in the House, in the Spring of 1896, the "educational test" bill which, he said, was principally prepared and specially advocated by the Immigration Restriction League of Boston. He pointed out then that the exclusion effected by the test of illiteracy would affect chiefly the immigration from the Mediterranean ports, and argued that this exclusion was desirable on the ground that the influx from those ports was "from races not suited to our civilization" because "radically different from us in education, habits of life and institutions of government." Moreover, this objectionable class of immigration, not kindred nor readily assimilating, did not go "to our unoccupied territory, but settled down in our large cities, in our congested districts. They add to the labor problems that are vexing them, and most of them go into the dangerous slums of our Eastern cities."

This objection has been amplified and more bluntly and bitterly urged in a current outcry against Italian immigration. It is urged that the Italian race stock is inferior and degraded; that it will not assimilate naturally or readily with the prevailing "Anglo-Saxon" race stock of this country; that intermixture, if practicable, will be detrimental; that servility, filthy habits of life, and a hopelessly degraded standard of needs and ambitions have been

17

ingrained in the Italians by centuries of oppression and abject poverty; that they are incapable of any adequate appreciation of our free institutions and the privileges and duties of citizenship; that the greater part are illiterate and likely to remain so; that they are lowering and will inevitably lower the American standard of living and labor and citizenship; that they are crowding out American laborers from avenues of employment; that their labor is no longer needed here for the development of the country; that a large percentage are paupers or on the verge of pauperism, and that the inevitable influence of their influx is pauperizing; that they make the slums in our large cities; that they burden our charitable institutions and prisons; and that there is no material evidence of progress and prospect of relief without the enforcement of a wide ranging exclusion.

In view of these charges and assumptions it seemed desirable to investigate the causes and flow of immigration and the advance of Italian settlement in this country by wide ranging correspondence and close personal observation. The facts thus gathered with the simple intention of candid inquiry and accurate statement are submitted for consideration in the following chapters, to which the authors associated in this presentation have contributed from their special investigations. They present in succession an examination of the Italian race stock, existing Italian characteristics and conditions of life in Italy, the

The Flow of Emigration

causes and regulation of immigration, its advance in the cities and agricultural districts of this country, its effect upon the standard and opportunities of American labor and the course of national development, its alleged pauperizing and criminal tendencies, and the sum of Italian accomplishment and rational hope of progress here as an integral part of the fusing of stocks in the complex American. ELIOT LORD.

CHAPTER II

THE INHERITANCE AND PROGRESS OF UNITED ITALY

The poorest Italian that comes to this country is joint-heir to a splendid heritage. Unfortunately for him, it does not fill his pockets nor better his rating in the returns of official inspectors. But it might justly advance him to higher consideration in the eyes of the American people. Every student of history must know it already, yet it is so rarely held up to view in the midst of current flouts and "Anglo-Saxon" conceits, that I venture to recall its ineffaceable outlines.

The far-reaching ancestry of the natives of South and Central Italy runs back to the dawn of the earliest Greek civilization in the peninsula and to the Etruscan, driving bronze chariots and glittering in artful gold when the Angles, Saxons and Jutes, and all the wild men of Northern Europe were muffling their nakedness in the skins of wild beasts, and making their lair in rock caverns or the rudest of huts. In the seat of his forefathers of purest Latin origin was laid the foundation of the traditional kingdom of Romulus and its offspring, the Roman Republic and Empire, outstretching its arms and its glory from the German ocean to the deserts of Africa, and from the Pillars of Hercules to the Euphrates.

If Sicily had for centuries no more share in the dominance of Rome than any other conquered province—and if the greater part of the inhabitants of Italy were dependent confederates and not Roman citizens—nevertheless, Italy was the homestead of the masterful Republic and Empire, and bore the most signal and lasting impress of their attainments and grandeur. And in the evolution of liberalism, the time came, it will be remembered, when all the free inhabitants of the Empire were declared to be Roman citizens and equal heirs to the glory of Rome.

Even when the crumbling Empire succumbed to barbarian invasion and could no longer protect the confines of its homestead, the languishing force of its civilization was still potent to mould the invaders. Ostrogoth and Visigoth, German and Frank alike, paid homage to the majesty of helpless Rome. Alaric lays greedy hands on the spoils of the Imperial city, but his successor, Athaulf, yields to the spell of the shadowy sceptre of empire and cloaks his invasion of Spain in the guise of a Roman official, obediently proceeding to the recovery of an old Roman province.

Odoacer, chief of the German mercenaries, when the line of Western emperors comes to an end, still professes his allegiance to Zeno, head of the reunited Empire by the voice of the Roman Senate, and is content to rule in Italy with no loftier title than the vague investiture of Patrician. When Theodoric, King of the Visigoths, wrests Italy from Odoacer (489 A.D.), a warrant is sought and obtained in the commission of the same emperor, Zeno.

Three centuries later, Pepin, King of the Franks, saves Rome from the threat of the Lombards, and shelters their dominion in Northern Italy. Still the title of "Patrician" is all that he ventures to claim and assert. When Constantine the Sixth is deposed and blinded in 797 A.D. by his mother Eirene, the unquenched haughtiness of Rome cries out that no woman can be Cæsar and Augustus, and makes Karl, son of Pepin, the great Charlemagne of mediæval romance, Emperor of the Romans. Pope Leo crowns him in the memorable year 800 A.D., and for more than a thousand years thereafter this traditional memorial of the glory of the old empire has been prized as an investiture without a peer, transcending the dignity of kings, and declaring a precedent, even if waiving an avowal of homage.

Not only was the imperial name still powerful to conjure with when it was no more than the graveclothes of the dust of empire, but even though invaders might protest their utter contempt of the enfeebled Italians and the Roman name, they were assimilated by resistless influences. Thus in the twelfth century, as Taine observes, the invading Germans under Frederick Barbarossa, "counting upon finding in the Lombards men of the same race as themselves, were surprised to find them so Latinized, having discarded the asperities of barbarian rudeness and imbibed from sun and atmosphere something of Roman finesse and gentleness, preserving the elegance of diction and the urbanity of antique customs, and imitating even to their cities and the regulation of public affairs the ability of the ancient Romans." *

Christianity was essentially the religion of the Empire after Constantine formally professed it in 323 A.D., and was carried by Roman influence even beyond the boundaries of the Imperial Dominion. Roman Law has been the foundation and frame of the Civil Law of Western Europe. The spoken language of Rome is not only the main source of modern Italian, but of Spanish, Provençal and French. Even in the land once part of the old Roman province of Dacia, the tongue of the people has the same root, and the inhabitants still claim their heritage in their names, Roumans.

For more than a thousand years after the days of Cæsar Augustus, the only books written in Western Europe were in Latin, and throughout the Middle Ages Latin was everywhere the chosen medium in the observances of religion and the preservation of learning. The literature of the Augustan Age has never ceased to be the study and inspiration of the world's scholars, and the

* Otho of Freysingen.

Latin language and classics have formed an integral part of all academic education.

What the old Roman civilization has been to the world we can faintly conceive, too, in view of the ruins of its cities—mines of treasures, invaluable to the historian and the artist, and marvellous even in their mutilation. Fosterer and perpetuator of so many enlightening and refining arts and pursuits, Roman civilization has made its impress so clear and deep on mediæval and modern ages that the world at large may well acknowledge its peculiar debt to the forefathers of modern Italy.

The transmission in Italy, moreover, of the Roman civilization was less impaired and more progressive, on the whole, than in any other country till the close of the sixteenth century. Italian coast cities grew to be the chief exemplars of commerce and the originators of banking. All memorials of ancient art and learning were cherished in museums and libraries. The chiefs of the clergy and the Italian nobility were often liberal patrons of artists.

Then, after a sluggish and dolorous period, there sprang up in Italy first the Renaissance—that glorious era of reviving fertility. In the midst of an epoch of pitiless wars and mortal enmities, St. Francis preaches a forgotten gospel of love. Then Greek and Latin antiquity, the Byzantine and Saracenic Orient—the Germanic and Italian middle age—"the entire past, shattered, amalgamated and transformed," says Taine, "seems to have been

24

melted over anew in the human furnace in order to flow out in fresh form in the hands of the new genius of Giotto, Arnolfo, Brunelleschi and Dante." Soon Italy is to become "the mother of the new learning—the home of the younger as of the older arts."

In the fifteenth century diplomacy had largely taken the place of force. With the coming of more peaceful days the useful arts sprang up like new grass after rain. The downtrodden peasant becomes a partner of his landlord, and divides with him the harvest. In Lombardy there is irrigation and rotation of crops. "Marble quarries," says Taine, "are worked at Carrara, and foundry fires are lighted in the Maremmes. We find in the cities manufactories of silk, glass, paper, books, flax, wool and hemp; Italy alone produces as much as all Europe, and furnishes to it all its luxuries." * * * "The Medicis possess sixteen banking houses in Europe; they bind together through their business Russia and Spain, Scotland and Syria. * * * They entertain at their court representatives of all the powers of Europe, and become the councillors and moderators of all Italy."

Then Donatello decorates the Campanile with his statues and Ghiberti casts the two gates of the Baptistery on whose doors Pollaiolo, his pupil, models the marvellous quail, which "had only to fly." Then Dello and Verocchio and Ghirlandaijo, and all the splendid company of goldsmiths and bronze workers and sculptors and fresco painters prepare the way for the perfect flowering of the fine arts of the Renaissance in Leonardo da Vinci, Michael Angelo and Raphael.

Thus Italy, in the phrase of Hamilton Mabie, became "the liberator and teacher of modern Europe." "No country owes more to her for its impulse than 'Anglo-Saxon' England," as Mr. Mabie once more recalls. The foremost early English poets and dramatists—Chaucer, Wyatt, Surrey, Spencer, Greene, Webster, Ford and Cyril Tourneur—show distinctively the Italian molding in poetry and drama. Even the master minds of greatest native force and fertility, Bacon and Shakespeare, would frankly acknowledge their debt. "Shakespeare's most romantic heroines, Juliet and Desdemona," observes Wilfred Scawen Blunt in The Speaker, "were both borrowed, as we know, and not without the loss of dignity from Bandello's Italian originals." Dante, Petrarch, Boccaccio and Ariosto became English household words through translations and imitations. From the dawn of early English art and literature, Italy has been a Mecca for her artists and scholars. The lofty imagination of Milton first expanded in Italian air. Here, too, the restless and embittered heart of Byron sought solace. All that is mortal of Shelley and Keats lies under the shadow of Rome. In Florence the genius of Browning reached its zenith, and his memorial tablet in Venice bears the lines of his poem—"Open my heart and you will see,

Graved inside of it, 'Italy.'" The influence of the leader, even in decadence, was deathless.

And can America forget her distinctive indebtedness? The New World owes to Italy the debt of the Old and more. May she not well remember that it was the son of a Genoese wool comber whose unflagging spirit revealed her existence to Europe—that the Florentine, Amerigo Vespucci, was her god-father—and that the voyages of the Cabots and Verrazano first traced the North American coast line and cleared the way for pioneer immigration. There must be a strange lack of memory and of recognition of service when prejudice against Southern Latin origin would put up an irrational bar of entry in the face of the countrymen of Columbus.

It is true that the Italy of the nineteenth century was very different in its comparative standing from the Italy of the sixteenth century. Then, in the view summarized in Freeman's "General Sketch of History," "it might be called the centre of Europe in that it had more to do with the rest of the world than any other country. It was the country to which others looked up as being at the head in arts, learning and commerce; and it was the country, too, where, just as in old Greece, there was the greatest political life among the many small states." For three centuries past a great part of the country had been standing still and large provinces even retrograding. In the general advancement of Europe, unhappy and distracted Italy had been outstripped, her ambitions stifled, and her people of the South, at least, crushed under burdens that sapped their energies and barely left sufferable their struggle for existence. Even her persistent dream of liberty and union had been the mock of the scoffer. The sneer of Metternich was the more bitterly galling in its near approach to the truth; "Italy is only a geographical expression."

Yet, in the face of this jeer, United Italy has uprisen in fact from the medley of jarring and dejected states. Her ideal has overcome foreign domination and internal discords. Her redemption is sure. Her union grows every year more intimate and perfect. Her old divisional names of Sicilian, Neapolitan, Tuscan and Lombard are sinking out of sight in the fused Italian.

In ancient times, at the opening of historical record, there were various racial divisions in Italy more or less strongly marked; Gallic and Ligurian in the North, Etruscan, Latin and Oscan in the Central Provinces, and Greek probably predominating in Southern Italy and Sicily. Yet all of these stocks were derived from the primitive Aryan of all the Western nations of Europe and their assimilation under Rome's unifying influences was continually progressive. In modern Italy there is no materially divergent strain of blood except in the Albanians and the Greeks of the South, and the Arabic elements in Sicily and Sardinia.

The frequent foreign invasions have not materially affected this prevalent strain. Existing variations in character and habits of life are chiefly attributable to varying political divisions, occupations and climate. Ever since the fall of the Empire until the recent unification, Italy has been merely a medley of jealous states and diverse forms of government, and these governments often mutable, if only in the exchange of one set of oppressors for another. In Central Italy especially there were minute sub-divisions into city states with independent life, policy, customs and social distinctions.

Unification for the past thirty years has been gradually fusing or obliterating these divisional lines, but no such brief term of years could possibly effect their extinction. The first comprehensive advance of unification was the establishment of a single form of central and local governments and the application of a single body of laws. The Piedmontese legislation and administration were extended to the whole of Italy to meet the vital need of the preservation of the union. Thenceforth intelligent public spirit has blocked the formation of any party domination based on sectional division lines. The general plan of education, administration of justice and taxation are based on the like unity of system. One of the most important advances toward fusion has been the extension in every practicable way of a common language—a standard Italian in place of the many provincial dialects. Common school education is effecting this throughout the country; the increased circulation of newspapers and books is promoting it, and there is a powerful impulse toward this unification in the military service of the nation. Conscripts are taught to speak Italian instead of dialects, and to read and write the common medium.

Pronounced diversities still exist also in provincial differences of occupation and degrees of progress. The North of Italy has long been the most progressive section through the comparative freedom of its institutions, the diversification of its industries and the spirit of its people. This division of the kingdom is notably active, industrious and prospering. The latest exposition at Turin was a signal illustration of the attainments of Italy in the leading industrial arts. Problems of the development of this progressive section are relatively insignificant. It is in Central and Southern Italy that the chief dragweights are encountered.

Compared with the South, Central Italy is already hopefully advanced. There is still too little variation of industry, but agriculture, the dominant interest, is prosecuted with high intelligence. The peasant farmer in Tuscany and largely in all Central Italy operates on the share or mezzeria system—dividing equally the products of his fields with his landlord. He comprehends fully the utility of the variation of crops. He raises wheat or other cereals, grapes and olives on the same podere. He knows the capacity of his land thoroughly. He has commonly introduced irrigation where necessary. He is exceedingly capable in the conduct of his plantations and supplements his crop products by keeping pigs and poultry, breeding calves and sometimes rearing silkworms. The women of his family usually add to his income by spinning and plaiting straw.

In Southern Italy the diversification of industry is, as yet, scarcely attempted and feeble at best. Agriculture is practically the sole reliance outside of the noxious sulphur mines of Sicily. The prevailing system of operation of the land is of large estates cultivated by hired labor. These properties are usually minutely subdivided and sublet. In the greater part of this region wheat is almost the only product. Rent and taxation are very burdensome. Resort to modern improvements is very rarely undertaken by landlords. The lot of both regular and irregular day laborers is miserable, and is often rendered appalling by the failure of the prevailing wheat crop or by the ravages of insects, disease or blight in the vineyards and olive groves.

Under such conditions no rapid advance can be looked for. Yet, despite all drawbacks, agriculture throughout Italy has been making certain progress. The use of artificial fertilizers is increasing. Variation and rotation of crops are extending. The export of agricultural products is advancing, though the temporary shock to the agricutural industry through the enactment of French protective tariffs was greatly depressing.

Nearly two million acres of malarious marsh lands have been cleared and rendered productive. An annual "Arbor Day" has been instituted, and the government is moving vigorously for the protection and increase of the forests maintaining the essential water supplies. For the preservation of the vineyards from the ravages of the phylloxera, grafting from the immune grape stocks of California is now largely prosecuted. Thus drought and disease are now intelligently combated, and relief has even been obtained from the scourge of hail, so often destructive to the crops of Northern Italy, by prodigious discharges of pyrite powder, converting the freezing drops to fine snow or sleet.

The remarkable advance of all manufacturing industries in Northern Italy is moreover enriching and stimulating to the kingdom as a whole. It is expanding the home market for agricultural produce and promoting its diversification. The range of manufacturing establishments is also further progressing down the peninsula into Central and even Southern Italy. In the past eighteen years the silk production of the kingdom has doubled and the weaving is now done at home instead of abroad. The cotton industry has advanced still more remarkably, expanding more than six fold in the last thirty years. Woollen manufactures are also profitably progressing, and surprising attainments have been reached in the development of iron and steel industries and the extension of electric plants of

CAV. A. SBARBORO
A Founder of the Italian-Swiss Colony, Asti, California

all kinds. For the production and application of the new world's force, electricity, the available water powers of Italian rivers have already done much to offset the lack of coal fields. No line of development is more congenial to Italian genius or commands more ready public appreciation.

Italy was among the first in Europe to undertake the construction and operation of electric railways. The Lugano line was operated with electrical equipment over part of its route as early as 1890. Now two other roads, the Lecco railway and the Varese railway, use electricity for their regular service, and other electric lines are in course of construction. The application to the movement of heavy traffic is particularly favored, and it is reasonable to expect progressive advances along this line of transportation.

Decadent shipbuilding is now again actively prosecuted also. The steamers operated as Italian lines have more than doubled in number within the past ten years, and all the vessels for these lines are now built in Italian ports. Genoa is already the second port of the Mediterranean in commercial importance, and with the opening of the Simplon Tunnel it is likely to become the chief port and surpass even its ancient commercial prestige.

The development of the mineral wealth of the kingdom is beginning to keep pace with the advances of its manufactures and commerce. Sardinia and Elba, from the days of the old Roman Empire, have been known to be rich in iron, lead and zinc, and the sulphur mines of Sicily and the Romagna have been worked from time immemorial. The province of Grosseto has large deposits of iron ore and cinnabar, and the known occurrences of copper, manganese and antimony in various parts of the country point to the practicability of extending developments. More than fifteen hundred mines are now in active operation, tripling the number reported in the first census after the unification of the kingdom, and the value of their annual output has risen to over $15,000,000.

The total value of the paid-up capital of railways, shipping companies, commercial and manufacturing establishments in the year 1904 is reckoned to be approximately four hundred million dollars, showing that this aggregate capital has doubled since the unification of the kingdom.

The standards of living have risen, too, throughout the country; wages have advanced on an average, at least, one-third; food is more plentiful; clothes are better, and both food and clothing are cheaper. The poverty of the people has not been a measure of their thrift, but of their opportunities. This is clearly demonstrated in the remarkable expansion of savings banks, and the so-called people's or small shareholders' banks. The first savings bank in Italy was opened in 1822, but it is only within the last twenty years that its multiplication was largely practicable. In 1900 the Italian savings banks, including those of the Post Office, numbered over five thousand,— the aggregate deposits were roundly four hundred million dollars, and the annual increase of late years has been over ten million dollars. The number of depositors in 1900 was five million, three hundred thousand. In addition to these are the people's banks, loaning money at low rates of interest to their shareholders, chiefly small business and peasant proprietors. These numbered 7200 in 1897, and their total of deposits was nearly seventy-five million dollars.

Co-operative, mutual aid and insurance societies have also multiplied very rapidly in the past two decades, and their obvious benefits have been a great stimulus to the extension of like societies among the Italians in America, a most substantial guarantee against the burdening of our public charitable institutions. General education has advanced also notably, though in parts of the kingdom this is still regretably backward. Still the percentage of illiteracy had fallen from fifty-seven per cent. in 1871 to thirty-seven per cent. in 1896. There were in 1900 over fifty thousand communal and nine thousand private schools.

The elementary schools, as a body, are as yet far below a satisfactory standard; the school buildings are poor and cramped, and the teachers ill paid. But in the extension of her technical and industrial schools Italy has a right to take pride. More than twenty years ago the government appointed a commission to study educational methods in detail. The commission reported that a broad and liberal support of industrial education on the part of the State would be the most effective means of advancing the interests of the country and raising the general condition of the people. It has lately been observed by United States Commercial Agent Harris that there is perhaps no country in the world to-day which has more extended home industries than Italy, and in the preparation of the government scheme of industrial education the house industries were particularly considered. The silk industry, the manufacture of hemp and tow, the twisting of baskets and braiding of straw hats furnish employment to many thousands of people in their own homes, and by the promotion of these industries Italy has succeeded in preventing a drift of population from the rural districts to the large cities. During the past twenty years a system of industrial schools has been gradually established, which now extends all over the country until every village which has an industry of any kind has a school for its advancement. In addition to these schools, advanced industrial schools have been established to give special training to students who expect to associate themselves with the glass, iron and marble, and other leading industries, and a certificate or diploma from one of these schools admits an applicant without further examination to the technical and classical universities of Italy.

The Inheritance and Progress of United Italy

The noted increase of the savings bank deposits of the kingdom is a gratifying proof of the widening distribution of prosperity. Yet this showing is only a fraction of the actual increase, as the poorer Italians are accustomed to hoard their savings in their homes like the French, and their appreciation of banks is not yet general. The working capital of the kingdom has become materially greater; the amount of money in circulation per capita has increased; individual holdings in land and personal property have been advanced, and the rising ability of the nation to meet its obligations is shown by the increase of returns without any increase of taxation until the income of the kingdom exceeds its expenditures.

Thus the progress of United Italy—painfully toiling upward under her inherited burden over an untried and perplexing path—has been truly remarkable and full of promise for her future, if the patience and perseverance of her people, in the solution of her problems, do not falter. Every succeeding year brings increased strength to bear her load, if it does not actually lighten it. What may not a people attain, of whom the keen observer Emil Reich bears witness in his discussion of " The Future of the Latin Races " in the Contemporary Review? "There can be little doubt," he says, " that they are the most gifted nation in Europe. What characterizes them above all is their initiative. It is the first step which is the hardest to take, but it is the Italians who have been ready to take the first step in action, and able to take the first step in the new paths of science. * * * We cannot help being impressed by their extraordinary mental activity and by the diversity of their attainments, which is almost incredible."

Certain it is that under the fortunate leadership of a sovereign, intelligent, progressive and patriotic, Italy is steadily exalting her rank among the nations of Europe.

ELIOT LORD.

CHAPTER III

Forty years ago, as has been noted, there was no immigration from Italy of any consequence, and the suggestion would have been generally derided that any serious problem of immigration was likely to arise. In the closing year of our Civil War it is observed in the "Italian Journeys" of Howells, that it is "difficult to tempt from home any of the homekeeping Italian race." There was then no perceptible movement of emigration anywhere, and it was an occasion of particular note by him that the only advertisement for the opening of emigration he had ever seen in Italy was the bulletin of a single German steamship company in the inconsiderable town of Colico.

Luigi Villari has accounted for this condition by the further observation of a widely disseminated prejudice against emigration. It was regarded as essentially unpatriotic by most of the movers of public opinion for an Italian to turn his back even temporarily to the crying demands of his own country, and to seek relief from its burdens in foreign lands. Italian writers, in fact, as

Villari notes, "have likened emigration to suicide, and every Italian who left his own country was regarded as little better than a traitor."

Thus it was, probably, that, in spite of the distressful conditions of the discordant Italian states, the movement of emigration was so inconsiderable before the unification of Italy was effected. With the attainment of freedom and unity a controlling appeal to patriotic endurance lost its force. There was further a more general and vivid comprehension of the widespread opportunities open to emigrants through the awakening of animation and intelligence and hope by the assured deliverance from dis-cord and oppression. Hence the distressful conditions impelling a movement of emigration began to operate with much less restraint.

The main underlying cause then inciting emigration was the pressure of population upon the means of subsistence. In spite of despotic oppression, foreign invasion and internal dissension, the population of Italy at the time of the unification was nearly double what it was at the beginning of the eighteenth century. The census of 1881 showed a population of 257 to the square mile, and thus was obviously fast advancing; for, twenty years later, in spite of the great efflux, the population had increased to 32,475,253, or 294 to the square mile.

There was no diversification or development of industry

throughout the greater part of the kingdom to keep pace with this increase. Except in the Northern Provinces there was practically no industry deserving the name outside of agriculture, and that pursued in a fashion little changed since the days of the Medici. Less than fifty years ago there was not a railroad in Sicily, and in all the Neapolitan provinces the total length of railways was a scant one hundred and fourteen miles. Tuscany had only 284 miles of railway at the opening of the year 1860; Lombardy, 100 miles less; and even in the comparatively thriving provinces of Piedmont and Liguria the extent of railways was then only 744 miles. Postal telegraph service was equally backward, and in Lower Italy there was not even a current of trade.

Moreover, the monopoly of the land in the hands of aristocratic proprietors was a discouraging obstacle to the advancement of the condition of the people in the agricultural districts by a distribution of the land among the peasant proprietary. Even when small holdings were secured independently in exceptional cases, they could hardly be maintained under a burden of taxation from which the poorest landholder could obtain no relief. There was no exemption for any kind of real estate, and the weight of taxation, even after the reconstruction of Italy, continued to fall disproportionately on the agricultural sections. Thus Prof. Panteleone observed in the Giornale degli Economisti in 1891 that Northern Italy, with 48 per cent. of the national wealth, was paying 40 per cent. of the taxation; central Italy, with 25 per cent., was paying 28 per cent., and Southern Italy, with not over 27 per cent., was paying 32 per cent. of the taxation. This was in face of the fact, too, that the rupture of the commercial treaty with France had very greatly stimulated the manufacturing interests in Piedmont and Lombardy, while the agricultural provinces had lost their chief market in France, and were burdened additionally by the increase in price of the manufactured goods which they had to purchase.

Moreover, the taxes were so assessed that the small landholder often feared to improve his estate lest the tax should be raised exorbitantly. The so-called family tax, imposed by the communes, was particularly obnoxious from the inquisition of its conduct and its varying with localities and individual official judgment, certainly unequal and often corrupt or unfair. No form of taxation is more irritating than one that pries into a household through official inspectors, counting rooms, examining furniture and carpets, then going through the stable and farmyard and making a tally and valuation of the live stock of every description without passing over even a few clucking hens, embracing the harness and tools and equipment of every description, and then checking up the returns by cross-questioning servants and neighbors. In many communes of Southern Italy, too, as Villari states, the discrimination appears to be peculiarly grinding, as the landlord's saddle horse is exempt, while a tax is assessed on the peasant's donkey.

The milling monopoly and the government monopolies of salt and tobacco have been particularly irksome also to the poor man, and his resentment is embittered by the daily parade of armed guards patroling the coast to prevent people from stealing sea water in buckets to obtain the salt. There is an attempted relief from the aggravation of these burdens through the protectionist policy strictly adhered to by the government of United Italy, yet the heavy duties on the large quantities of foodstuffs, which are necessarily imported to supply the demands of the people, have made even this protection largely a burden whose weight is the most grievous to those least able to bear it.

Since the unification of Italy the national administration has unquestionably been making truly patriotic efforts to deal adequately with existing conditions and provide methods of relief, but it has confessedly been laboring under a perplexing strain. Relief from the dragweight of taxation was seemingly essential to a hopeful advance in Central and Southern Italy, at least; but, in spite of the intelligently liberal policy of the Ministry, adequate relief has not yet been effected. This is largely owing to what is esteemed the necessity of maintaining military armaments on land and sea rivalling the establishments of the greater nations of Europe. To this drain has been coupled the extraordinary expenses entailed by a progressive policy of internal development which, in part, has been charged with extravagance and misjudgment. These developments necessarily overran for the time the immediate returns of income, so that both the military and civil policy have made the taxation of the kingdom exceedingly burdensome.

A leading historian of Italy, Pasquale Villari, gloomily observes in his discussion of "Present Day Problems in Italy," in Nuova Antologia of 1899, that in proportion to the wealth of the kingdom it is the most heavily taxed and deeply indebted country of Europe. In wealth, he notes, Italy has not a quarter part of the possessions of France, but contributes about half as much to the expenses of the State. It pays more than a million francs daily as interest on its funded debt alone. Its annual revenue is 1,600,000,000 lire. Half of this is swallowed up by interest on debts of various kinds, including the pension list. Adding 160,000,000 lire devoted to the collection of revenue, there remains but little more than 600,-000,000 lire for all national expenses, including the army, navy, public works, prisons, police and general administration. Existing taxes he considers to be inadequate, burdensome and antiquated. Objects of luxury pay next to nothing, and almost all necessities of life are heavily taxed. The poor man pays fifty per cent. of the sum levied by government. New debts, he concludes, "are impossible; new taxes, only more so; economy is our only resource."

In opposition to this view must justly be ranged the more hopeful outlook ably presented by Dr. G. Tosti in the American Journal of Sociology (Vol. VIII, No. 1), 1902, under the caption "The Financial and Industrial Outlook of Italy." This competent examiner points out that despite impressions to the contrary, Italian financial policies have been so ably planned and handled that there has been a continuous rise in the value of Italian State bonds on foreign markets, and a constant diminution in the rate of exchange. Moreover, as observed by Mr. Gino C. Speranza in his contribution to the issue of Charities (May 7th, 1904), United Italy has never admitted the possibility of bankruptcy, never paid her national debt in paper in spite of the "tremendous demands made upon her youth." Her industrial and social progress since unification, in spite of all handicaps, is undeniable, too, as detailed in the preceding chapter. There has been an influx of capital, even in the most depressed regions, of very material consequence through the contributions of emigrants, and the demand for labor at home, its wages and the openings for employment have assuredly advanced. In the important measure of progress afforded by the rate of wages alone, improvement is beyond dispute, and Adolfo Rossi particularly credits as a good effect of emigration the increase of wages all over Italy from one-third to one-half.

In his expert discussion of the effect of emigration on Italy in Charities (May 7th, 1904), Signor Rossi further emphasizes the marked difference in recent years in the causes of emigration from Italy. "It is not hard conditions," he observes, "or starvation that now sends Italians to America; they come because they are eager for more money. A mason earning 4 lire a day in Southern Italy can live there comfortably, but he has heard that he can earn 6 a day in America"; so he emigrates, and the emigration has swelled so rapidly that the available labor supply has greatly diminished, and there is now a keen competition in parts of Italy for laborers with the inevitable increase of wages.

In spite of this advance and its tendency to check emigration, local conditions may operate to stimulate it temporarily. This was particularly so during the last year (1904) and the year preceding, when the agricultural industry was depressed by crop failures, the ravages of the phylloxera and the falling prices of citrus fruit.

Early in 1903 it was reported that 908 provinces in Italy had been invaded by the phylloxera, and that not less than 750,000 acres of vineland had been entirely destroyed. This insect entered Italy first in 1879, nine years after its appearance in France, and the extent of its devastation is attributed to the fact that it has not been repressed as effectively by the introduction of American grafts. When the insect stings an American vine or one protected by grafting, the opening immediately fills with sap and closes leaving no wound. Hence it is now deemed essential to protection against this insect in Europe that the vine shall be Americanized, and the California grafts are generally preferred.

The citrus fruit plantations have been suffering from the depression for which there is no immediate prospect of relief. It was reported last year by Alexander Heingartner, U. S. Consul at Catania, that lemons were hard to market at 3 lire (58 cents) per thousand on the trees, which only a few seasons ago commanded 15 lire ($2.90) per thousand. Through immense mass meetings, the government had been importuned to obtain favorable treatment of citrus products in new commercial conventions and to obtain, if practicable, better tariff rates from the United States and Russia. New and modern lines of navigation, especially to Australia, were requested, and lower freight rates by sea and rail. There was also an insistent pressure for the abolition of the present octroi tax on fruit.

The province of Piedmont is the most productive cocoon section of the kingdom, but the crop for 1903 was only about one-third of the average, owing to the late frost which kept the mulberry trees almost leafless. In default of the natural food of the silkworm, other expedients were tried to keep the worms alive, but none succeeded, so that the disaster was very grievous, as the Consul at Turin reported in July, 1903. The failure of this crop, and the injury of the wheat, grape and other crops of the province by the frost and prolonged rain were so discouraging to the peasants that a great increase in the emigration from this province was anticipated during 1904.

It is of interest to note that in spite of these inciting causes the emigration from Italy to this country not only did not increase, as compared with the showing of the year ending June 30, 1903, but on the other hand, a marked diminution is noted, as well as an unprecedented return of emigrants to Italy.

ITALIAN REGULATION OF EMIGRATION

It is of no practical concern to inquire into the grounds of complaint of the insufficiency of the emigration laws and the laxity of their enforcement when Italy was a medley of discordant and largely misgoverned states. It is immaterial, too, whether any deficiencies existed in the formative years immediately following the unification of the present kingdom.

From the year 1888, which practically marks the beginning of the considerable flow of immigration to this country, examination shows that no nation of Europe has been more circumspect in its provisions for regulating and safeguarding its emigration and colonization.

The Causes and Regulation of Italian Emigration

The law passed by the Italian parliament and approved by the king on the 31st of December, 1888, was carefully considered and designed to assure in every detail, the judicious oversight and control of emigration. Its specifications were supplemented by special instructions and departmental regulations assuring the administration and enforcement of the law with certainty and efficiency.

Emigration from the kingdom was declared to be free, subject only to the specific obligations imposed upon citizens by the law of the State and the restrictive laws of foreign countries. To provide against the unrestricted depletion of the number of male citizens available for the defence of the State, military of the first and second categories on indefinite leave, belonging to the regular army or to the movable militia, were prohibited from emigration without the permission of the Minister of War.

No one, without violation of law, could collect emigrants, sell or distribute tickets for emigration, or procure or assist their embarkation, unless formally commissioned by the Minister of the Interior as Emigration Agent, or licensed by the Prefect of a province, as subagent.

To obtain the commission of Emigration Agent, the applicant must be at least twenty-one years of age, and a resident citizen of Italy; he must not have lost his civil rights, nor be under surveillance in the interest of public security, nor have been condemned for any crime against the good faith of the public, nor in relation to trade or commerce, or good custom, nor against persons or property, nor for infractions of the emigration law or regulations. An agent receiving a commission was required to deposit from 3,000 to 5,000 lire in bonds of the State as security for his observance of the law and regulations, and any claims on behalf of an emigrant for which he might become liable.

A duly commissioned agent was authorized to appoint sub-agents in accordance with the law, but no sub-agent could act without obtaining a special license from the Prefect of the province in which the agent was stationed, and any further delegation of powers to assist emigration was prohibited. No agent or sub-agent could promote, in any way, the collection of emigrants outside of the district in which he was authorized to act, and it was expressly provided that it should not devolve upon the emigrant to pay the agent or sub-agent for any services whatever, except to reimburse them for the actual sums expended on his account.

For determining identity and compliance with the regulation and prohibitions of the law, a contract in triplicate must be made in every case between the agent, sub-agent and emigrant, or, if the latter was a minor, his guardian. One copy of this contract must be given to the emigrant and one to the captain of the port, the agent retaining the third. If any emigrant should be unable to write his name, this contract must be signed by the mayor or by an authority of public security.

This contract must specify the name, age, profession and last residence of the emigrant.

The date of his discharge from the army or the permission of the Minister of War.

The place of departure and the place or port of destination.

The time of departure.

The name of the transporting vessel and the post assigned to the emigrant, with the express prescription of the space assigned to him in conformity with the regulation of the law of 1879.

The period of stoppage at intermediate ports, when the voyage was not made directly, and in case of change, the name and character of the new vessel.

The total or partial price of the expenses of subsistence on board, with the proviso that this stipulation must in no case be inferior to the ration established by the law of 1879.

The quantity of baggage which the emigrant was allowed to take with him.

Explicit provision was made in the law to protect the emigrant from any imposition or abuse on the part of any concerned in his passage to any foreign country; and any agent, owner, captain, master or charterer of transporting vessels were subject to a penalty, both of fine and

imprisonment, for receiving emigrants on board without the contract and permit above noted.

Any infraction of the main regulations of the law by
the agent or sub-agent of emigration was punishable
with a like penalty.

For further security the regulations for the execution
of this law constrained the procurement of the visé of the
police authorities of the port of embarkation in order to
make the contract valid as a passport for emigration, and
these authorities were instructed to limit the passports in
every case to the regulated capacity of the transporting
vessel.

Agents were expressly prohibited, also, from furnishing
passage to persons who were not allowed to enter the
foreign country to which they proposed to go, and were
bound to conform to all rules laid down by the Ministry
for the protection of emigrants, auxiliary to the regulations adopted by the governments of foreign countries
receiving the immigration.

To direct and control, as far as practicable, the flow of
emigration, correspondence was opened by special ar-
rangement between the Ministry of the Interior and the
Italian consular service. The consuls were called upon
to re-examine carefully the basis of their former reports
on immigration to the Ministry of Foreign Affairs, and
to forward as complete additional information as possible,
covering:

The Causes and Regulation of Italian Emigration

1. The physical, hygienic and agricultural conditions of the districts in which they were stationed, and all other conditions having relation to colonization and population.

2. The number of Italian immigrants already located in each district.

3. The industries, trades and occupations in which the immigrants were generally engaged.

4. The laws enacted concerning these immigrants and the relations sustained by them to the authorities, land-holders and contractors.

5. The pay which they receive and the prices of provisions.

6. Whether the means of communication were good and whether there were good markets in the neighborhood for the sale of their productions.

7. Whether there were any immigration companies or any such in course of formation.

8. Whether land was granted to immigrants desiring to found a colony on it, and if so, on what terms; also whether land was sold to immigrants on easy terms, and if so, on what terms.

9. Whether the immigrants when they desired to return home met with obstacles in communication with the seaboard, or in their immigration or labor contract, or in the local laws and ordinances.

In this requisition from the Minister of the Interior, consuls were enjoined to send in regularly, twice a year thereafter, reports covering all these matters of inquiry and detailing any changes of note occurring in the conditions affecting immigration. They were particularly requested to give clear and accurate statements of the condition of immigrants, whether good or bad, without concealing anything out of regard to foreign governments. In the use or publication of the information received in the interest of the public, the Ministry undertook to maintain the greatest reserve compatible with the best interests of immigrants to avoid disclosure of its sources of information.

Twelve years later, after the provisions of this law had been thoroughly tested, supplementary legislation was enacted in the passage of the law of January 31, 1901. The design of this law was to remedy any defects noted in the operation of existing legislation, to institute the best feasible safeguards for the protection and guidance of emigrants, and especially to suppress any artificial promotion of emigration.

As an effective instrument of its purpose, it created a Government Board of Emigration by the institution of the Royal Emigration Department of Italy. This consists of a Commissariat and Council. The Commissariat is composed of a Commissioner-General and three Associate Commissioners, with a suitable provision of executive clerks. In co-operative and advisory association a council or Board of Emigration was established, consisting of the Commissioner-General; five delegates, representing the Departments of the Interior, Treasury, Navy, Public Instruction and Agriculture; three members appointed by royal decree from such persons as shall have made the science of geography, statistics and economy their special study; and two additional members—one nominated by the National League of Italian Co-operative Societies, and the other by leading Mutual Aid Societies of the chief towns of the kingdom.

The headquarters of this department were established at Rome with three main branches at Genoa, Naples and Palermo. In every municipality there is also an Advisory Committee, under the law, composed of the Syndic, the local justice, a physician, a representative of the clergy, and one of a trades organization or agricultural society. The duty of each committee is to advise and protect emigrants. The central body issues a special bulletin and circulars of instruction to these local committees. The bulletin and circulars contain the information sent in by the consuls abroad and by the Travelling Emigration Inspectors regarding emigration matters.

In a communication formally addressed by Adolfo Rossi, Visiting Inspector of this department, in the spring of 1904, to the President of the American Society for the Protection of Italian Immigrants, the purpose and operation of this amended Italian emigration legislation and its conduct under the supervision of the Royal Emigration

Department are defined with the weight of official authority. While the law of 1901, as Signor Rossi notes, does not question the right of expatriation and emigration, it hedges this right around with such special safeguards "that it may well be called a restrictive law." According to the intelligent view of Senator Bodio, the head of the Royal Emigration Department, as reported by Signor Rossi, "Legislatures and governments can neither create nor direct migratory currents, but only discipline. These are like the great marine currents which go to warm and improve distant lands, flowing in one direction until some natural change turns their flow elsewhere."

The main provisions of this discipline of regulation are thus summarized by Signor Rossi:

"First. It prohibits all steamship lines from using any methods of publicity calculated to encourage emigration. Whoever advertises by circulars, handbills, or other notices, matters tending to encourage emigration, or distributes the same, is subject to a heavy fine and imprisonment."

"Secondly. No steamer carrying immigrants can be enrolled as an emigrant ship under the law unless a Special Commission of Examiners issues a permit. Such permit can only be granted when the steamship company has complied with all the regulations fixed by the law regarding hygiene, safety, speed, and the allotment of proper space for berths. Even the quality and quantity of food is fixed by the law. Furthermore, no steamer can sail without undergoing two examinations, medical and administrative, to ascertain whether every provision of the law has been complied with."

"At the ports of Genoa, Naples and Palermo our officers inspect all lodging houses and immigrant hotels to see that the hygienic rules are obeyed, and that the law is obeyed regarding rates, food and lodging, which expenses for the two days preceding departure are payable by the steamship companies. Special officers meet the immigrants at the various railroad stations at the ports of departure, and escort them to the piers or lodging houses."

"Thirdly. Every steamship company must pay the expenses and salary of a Government Commissioner (generally a surgeon of the royal navy), who sails with each boat carrying immigrants, and whose duty is to look after hygienic conditions and the observance of the immigration law."

"Fourthly. No navigation company is allowed to sell tickets in Italy without previously filing a bond with the State, conditioned upon the compliance of the law."

"There is furthermore a tax of 8 f. which the steamship companies must pay on each ticket sold. All such taxes constitute a fund to be used exclusively for the benefit of immigrants. We see, therefore, that the law has imposed many burdens and expenses upon the navigation companies. To prevent too great an increase in ticket rates, or the formation of pooling agreements, it is provided that the Immigration Department shall fix the maximum of transportation rates every four months."

"The law also gives the right to the government to suspend immigration to any given country when special circumstances to the detriment of the immigrant arise. For example, two years ago, when it was ascertained that on account of the crisis in coffee plantations, the condition of Italian immigrants in San Paulo, Brazil, was critical, the government withdrew the permission given to Brazil for the free importation of Italians to the farms and plantations in that country. The law also provides special regulations regarding children and women, such as the prohibition of sending minors out of the country except under certain circumstances, etc."

"In three years' existence the department has not encouraged immigration toward any definite place. Indeed it has often been objected that the Immigration Department discourages immigrants from going to this and that country for this or that reason, and does not point out where they can go. If all immigrants were to follow its advice, they would all stay at home. There could be no higher definition of the policy of the department than this—which indeed proves that it is not an employment agency, but an institution seeking to prevent forced or artificial immigration, and to protect the immigrants from those who exploit them."

The Causes and Regulation of Italian Emigration

"When foreign governments or foreign contractors send us requests for Italian laborers, our Immigration Department refuses such request unless the wages offered are equal to the prevailing rate of wages of the demanding government or its contractors for such laborers. Our department is opposed to the use of Italian labor as a method of reducing prevailing rates abroad. Here are two examples: In 1902 the government of Cape Colony asked permission to import 500 Italian peasant families, offering 2 1/2s. a day wages, besides house, ground and wood."

"Such request was refused because I reported as the result of an investigation in Cape Colony that white farm laborers there earned more than the amount offered. Again in January, 1903, some mining companies of Johannesburg (Transvaal) asked for 1,000 Italian miners at 6s. per day. This also was refused, it having been ascertained that although negro miners received less than the amount offered, white miners received more. A few months ago, the same companies, needing foremen, sent a mining engineer to Italy, and our department granted the permit for them, after securing a written contract by which the companies bound themselves to pay such foremen 20s. a day, the wages paid to English foremen at Johannesburg."

"In conclusion let me say that the department which I have the honor of representing not only does not en-

courage immigration, but does everything in its power
to fight those who would force its increase. The most
recent example is this: Our law allowed steamship companies to have an agent in every commune in the kingdom,
but by an amendment of January 4, 1904, the number of
such agents is reduced to one for each company, and only
one for every group of twenty or thirty municipalities."

ELIOT LORD.

CHAPTER IV

The first employment at hand for the average Italian on landing in this country is offered in the cities of the Northern Atlantic coast or on the railway lines—steam and electric—linking the cities and towns. He cannot speak English and understands barely a few words, if any at all. He has only a few dollars in his pocket, and must have immediate paying occupation for his support. This he secures, through friends or agents of contractors, as a common laborer on roads, docks, trenches, basements and other public and private work. Padroni have driven hard bargains with him, taking advantage of his necessities. Many are no doubt still imposed upon, though a contractor's agent is entitled to a reasonable fee for his service, like any other broker. The immigrant has no more claim to free service than the client of any domestic labor agency.

The mass of the immigrants are classed as unskilled laborers, or without defined training. This classification is passably correct, but it should be borne in mind that the great majority of the immigrants from Italy have had some experience in gardening, farming, or home industries of some kind. The line is not so sharply drawn as in our country between the artisan and farm hand. Many of the working men in the towns have little fields or market gardens outside which they cultivate in off hours. Most of the farm hands live in towns, trudging often long distances to and from the lands they cultivate, and working at odd jobs in town when not otherwise employed. Even the workers in industries engaging their services without a break, like the miners and quarrymen, have usually small tracts of land for crops, vines or fruit raising. It is chiefly in Northern Italy that factory industries like ours have grown up, and workers are trained to the subdivision of labor and single specific employment.

There is a larger percentage of Italian skilled labor coming to this country than is popularly supposed, and more than is marked in the official returns of our Immigration Department, though the record of a single year, which may be taken as typical, shows a widely varied range of occupation. In the Annual Report of the Commissioner-General of Immigration for the fiscal year ending June 30, 1903, the occupations of aliens arriving during the year are classified. By this table it appears that 253 were entered from northern Italy as having professional occupations and 532 from Southern Italy. The distribution by professions was as follows:

Italian Settlement in American Cities

	From Northern Italy.	From Southern Italy.
Actors	13	4
Clergy	18	42
Editors	7	3
Engineers	42	23
Lawyers	4	5
Musicians	32	273
Physicians	17	24
Sculptors and artists	81	65
Teachers	18	51
Not specified	16	42
Total	253	532

In the various trades and industries the distribution was, viz.:

	Northern Italy.	Southern Italy.
Bakers	182	605
Barbers and hairdressers	2,057	2,088
Blacksmiths	236	913
Brewers	15	4
Butchers	51	265
Carpenters and joiners	396	2,583
Clerks and accountants	175	292
Engravers	5	7
Gardeners	62	262
Ironworkers	19	233
Jewellers	9	85
Locksmiths	13	9
Machinists	48	58
Mariners	259	1,790
Masons	1,251	2,975
Mechanics (not specified)	82	257
Millers	23	165
Miners	2,169	351
Painters and glaziers	63	15

	Northern Italy.	Southern Italy.
Plumbers	4	1
Printers	13	62
Saddlers and harness makers........	5	28
Seamstresses and dressmakers	222	2,398
Shipwrights	3	....
Shoemakers	326	4,636
Stone-cutters	436	542
Tailors	206	3,258
Tanners and curriers................	11	37
Tinners	15	77
Tobacco manufacturers.............	15	....
Watch and clockmakers.............	15	43
Weavers and spinners...............	226	348
Wheelwrights	3	16
Not specified......................	131	241
Total	6,766	24,895
Agents or factors..................	7	9
Bankers	1	2
Farmers	200	678
Farm laborers......................	8,462	32,391
Hotel keepers......................	12	17
Laborers	15,622	85,682
Merchant dealers and grocers........	422	872
Personal and domestic servants.....	1,956	6,606
Not stated........................	166	1,045
Total	24,848	127,302
MISCELLANEOUS.		
No occupations (including women and children).....................	5,562	43,388
Grand Total....................	37,429	196,117

In the Report of the Industrial Commission on Immigration—1901—a digest was printed of the industrial

Peach Orchard Scene, Near Centralia, Illinois. Italian Settlement

Italian Settlement in American Cities

statistics of the census of 1890, showing, among other records, the percentage of total numbers of males employed of each nationality in the principal industries entered by them. In this table Italy figures as follows:

	Per cent.
ITALY	100.00
Laborers not specified	34.15
Steam railroad employés	10.56
Miners and quarrymen	8.51
Merchants and dealers	6.53
Agricultural laborers	3.92
Hucksters and peddlers	2.96
Barbers and hairdressers	2.91
Boot and shoemakers	2.80
Tailors	1.99
Farmers and planters	1.89

The nationalities showing the largest percentage of unskilled labor in this compilation were respectively, Italy (34.15%), Hungary (32.44%), Ireland (25.16%), and French Canada (16.43%).

What is reckoned as unskilled labor is specially in demand for heavy outdoor or manufacturing work of the crudest kind, because the ambitious American-born workman has risen above this level and does not care to compete on it. The Italian immigrant is now perforce content to do it for the time until he has gained a better foothold in the country, but his children born here will not engage in it, and educated working men generally will not stoop to it. Among the Italian laborers on our street and railways are some clerks and artisans, and even professional men.   Their ignorance of our language constrains them to hard labor until they are able to make their services otherwise valuable to American employers.   In such work they can be readily directed by Italian foremen, and the average immigrant shrinks from exposing his ignorance to any but his own countrymen.   He has reason for this in the common lack of patience with his supposed dullness and blunders.   I have heard Americans, otherwise apparently rational, shout at Italians as if bellowing would make spoken English more intelligible, and swear at them as if ignorance of English was an unspeakable offence. The Italian is sensitive to ridicule, and feels the injustice of abuse keenly whether he resents it openly or not.   Hence he is slow to venture alone in a strange community or to seek employment on a farm where he will be isolated until he is able to speak English with considerable fluency, and has become well acquainted with American ways and requirements.   The clustering in cities, so often complained of, is attributable not only to his fondness for social life and lack of means to enter the country, but to the lack of invitation with any assurance of patience or sympathy.

In the early years of the Italian influx the newcomers were ready to take up any occupation which promised them a living.   In the wastes of an American city they saw an opportunity.   They multiplied the number of rag pickers and refuse sorters.   They extended the fruit markets and cut down the cost to the ordinary buyer by selling from handcarts and stands in every part of the city. The popular taste for fruit grew with its fuller display and convenience of purchase. So the number of street fruit dealers very greatly increased. The persistence of the Italian and his care in handling his stock gave him practically the control of this business until the competition of the Greek immigrants shook his monopoly. He can still contend on equal terms, but he has no special bent for peddling, and is disposed to engage in more active and laborious occupations, unless he can acquire a permanent paying stand, or a fruit store, or a green grocery. Thus the Greek has been pushing the Italian off the street and increasing the number of small fruit and grocery stores. Bootblacking is tiresome and grimy work, and steady, sinewy, patient workers like the Italians excel in it, as is shown by the Italian occupation of stands in all suitable locations. Italian barber shops have become numerous also, and attract general custom. Italian tailors, men and women, compete successfully in the larger workshops and in their rooms in lodging houses. In a recent canvass of a representative block in the Italian quarter in Philadelphia, housing 358 Italian families, the occupations of the heads of families listed according to the number engaged in each from the highest down were: common outdoor laborers, shopkeepers, rag pickers or rag dealers, tailors, peddlers and vendors, unskilled employees in factories and stores, barbers, street cleaners, cobblers, shoemakers and musicians. This marks the drift of the greater part of the Italian influx into the cities of the East in the early years of its settlement.

The advance of settlement in the cities is substantially alike in all cases. If Italians are employed in manufacturing establishments, they seek lodgings near their workshops to save carfare or long walks, if they can, and there may be clusters of Italian tenements for this reason in widely separated quarters of a city. But they are attracted first ordinarily to some particular precinct, ward or quarter from its cheap accommodation and their natural disposition to flock together in spite of their provincial prejudices. If laborers on railways or other works near a city are not lodged in temporary camps on the ground, they are likely to seek lodgings in the neighboring city and overcrowd for the time the Italian tenements.

Natives of the same community or district at home will prefer the same living associations here, if they can contrive to renew them. Hence a little new colony in a city is often composed almost exclusively of immigrants from the same district, and a larger settlement is made up of different district colonies. For years these colonies are likely to retain their distinctive habits and clannishness, but as their children grow up under fusing school influences and become Americanized, the original divisions fade away.

In spite of the jealousy of the Irish at the intrusion and

their free-spoken jibes at the " Dago," the first cluster of Italians in a city has commonly been in tenements where the Irish are thickest. They may divide a tenement, at first, but the Irish vacate it sooner or later. There is less clashing between the two nationalities than might be expected. This is largely attributable, probably, to the essential good nature of both. The common religion is also a bond of union, and Italians are usually attracted to Irish-American churches and parish schools while they are too few or too poor to establish churches of their own. The influences of a Catholic church organization are steadfastly bent against racial antagonisms, and for the promotion of the Christian fellowship of its followers. Its chief directors and many of its priests of all nationalities have been trained in Italian seminaries or have visited Italy more or less frequently, and all look to Rome as the prime seat of their church. Their knowledge of Italian foundations, customs and often of the language, and their sympathy with the people have made them greatly influential in the religious and broadly moral guidance of the immigrants. Hence, it has been a natural sequence for the Italians to follow the Irish into their churches, as into their tenements, and with the increase in their numbers to acquire the churches like the tenements.

Thus in New York, for example, the old Church of the Transfiguration on Mott Street, in a parish established in 1827, has passed from the Irish-Americans to the Italians. So, too, with the Church of our Lady of Pompeii in Bleecker Street, the successor of the Church of St. Benedict. Another prominent instance is the Church of St. Anthony in Sullivan Street, dedicated in 1866, when the congregation was mainly Irish-Americans, but transferred to the Italians through the spread of their settlement. This procedure has been so common in the course of Italian establishment that it is popularly remarked that the Irish build but the Italians inherit.

There is a well-grounded complaint of Italian city settlements that their tenements are insufferably packed. The average density of population in the Italian quarter of the North End of Boston was 1.41 to a room when the tenement-house census was taken in 1891, and there was little noted relief from the pressure at the end of the century. Conditions in Philadelphia were even worse and are still unrelieved. The latest census statistics show that the Second, Third and Fourth Wards, where nearly all the Italians live, contain more than one-sixteenth of the total population of the city in less than one one-hundred-and-fiftieth of the area.

In New York City the Fourth, Sixth, Eighth, Twelfth, Fourteenth, Fifteenth, Seventeenth and the Nineteenth Wards now contain by far the greater part of the Italian tenement-house population, though thousands of Italian families are distributed through other wards, chiefly from the Fifth to the Twenty-second, inclusive.

Italian Settlement in American Cities

The largest percentage of the entire Italian tenement-house population is shown in Wards Six and Fourteen. In the first-named 2,036 families of Italian parentage constitute 61.01 per cent. of the tenement-house population. In Ward Fourteen, extending from Broadway to the Bowery and from Canal to East Houston Street, there were 4,856 Italian tenement families, out of a total of 5,631, according to the recent report of the Tenement House Department; a percentage of 86.24. This is the highest percentage given for any ward in the city, though Ward Twelve exceeds all others in its number of Italian tenement families, according to the same official report. Here the Italian families number 5,220, but they constitute only 6.12 per cent. of the total tenement-house population. Block 1,442 in the Fourteenth Ward has the unenviable distinction of being the most densely populated in the ward, and containing the largest number of families of Italian parentage in the city. In this block 492 Italian families are lodged in the area extending north from Prince Street, between Mott and Elizabeth Streets.

In the city at large there were 29,623 families of Italian parentage, as the official report records, or slightly more than half the number of families (56,885), whose heads were American. In the total number of Italian resident families in tenements and other houses, Ward Twelve leads with a reported number of 6,121 in 1903, and Ward Fourteen is second with 5,641. This enumeration reck-

oned that the heads of families constituted 7.57 per cent.
of the total of the heads of families in the city.

The evils of congestion and wretched housing have
been graphically set forth by Jacob Riis, Kate Holladay
Claghorn, Emily Wayland Dinwiddie and other expert
observers. The shameful construction of tenements under
lax municipal regulations and oversight is chiefly responsible for the intolerable conditions still existing in New
York and other large cities. Certainly the Italian immigrant did not build such breeders of disease, death and
crime as are still tolerated in our larger cities. One row
of seven alley houses, recently observed by Miss Dinwiddie in Philadelphia, stands back to back with another row
so that all ventilation from the rear is cut off. Such
meagre sunlight and air as enter its windows strain through
a court four feet three inches wide. All day long lamps
are kept burning in these pestilential buildings where day
is barely distinguished from night.

The vileness of such lodgings is accented, no doubt, by
the insufferable overcrowding of tenants, which has been
tolerated. In his poverty and anxiety to cut down living
expenses, the Italian immigrant has too often disregarded
health and even decency. He needed the hand of official
restraint and still needs it. In the Italian quarter of
Philadelphia it is lately recorded that 30 Italian families,
numbering 123 persons, were living in 34 rooms. Here
is clearly a call for better and stricter municipal regulations

—and immigrants should not be suffered to struggle through such conditions, with grievous experience to themselves and the public.

It is to their credit, nevertheless, that so many are doing so well under the influences that hamper them. In a recent issue of "Americans in Process," a publication of the South End House in Boston, it is observed that " many of the Italians (in Boston) are beginning to seek something better. They are now in considerable numbers moving into the more desirable tenements to the west of Hanover Street; and some families, especially of the second generation, are taking a more significant step in detaching themselves from the colony and settling amid pleasanter surroundings." It is certain that many Italian families are now living in the outlying wards and suburbs of Boston, particularly in Winthrop, South Boston and Dorchester, in clean, comfortable houses.

In Philadelphia, also, it is remarked by Miss Dinwiddie that " a large proportion of the worst houses were occupied by recent immigrants who had not had time to work their way up to living in more expensive dwellings and did not know where to seek redress from the discomforts they suffered from in their present houses, if they knew or desired anything better." In short, there is no large city in the country in which Italian progress is not marked; and Italian advance in New York under the reformed condition of the tenement districts is particularly noteworthy.

Any sweeping classification of congested sections as the slums of a city is untenable. Congestion is necessarily a menace to health. It is socially undesirable. It is to be deplored and remedied by every feasible agency. But congestion does not make the slum, necessarily, with its essential characteristics of squalor, degradation and crime. The congested districts of New York, Philadelphia and other leading American cities to-day are not slums, though they doubtless contain slums. It is by its average character that a district must be judged and classified, and not by existing exceptions.

There is not an exalted standard of cleanliness in the congested quarters of New York or other great American cities, but they are not intolerably filthy, except in spots, and the inhabitants are not sunk in degradation beyond any rational prospect of betterment. Even in our most thickly congested city districts the greater part of the families are, at least, decently cleanly, and there is not a single district in which a regard for cleanliness and an observance of essential sanitary regulations are not steadily advancing under the pressure of improved systems of tenement-house inspection, the ordinances of public health boards, the efforts of progressive settlement workers, and the rising public appreciation of improved sanitation and cleanliness. The congestion in New York exceeds that of any other American city, yet any candid and close investigation of existing conditions in this city will unquestionably sustain these conclusions.

It may be unhesitatingly affirmed that all these sections are in better condition to-day—and very materially better—than they were at the time of original occupation by Italian immigrants. Conclusive testimony as to the cleanliness of Italian tenements is furnished by the inspectors of the Tenement House Department of New York City. They declare that tenements in the Italian quarters are in as good condition as any in the city, and much cleaner than those in the Jewish and Irish tenement districts. The Italian settlement has assuredly increased property values and bettered the average moral character of the districts. Malodorous Mulberry Street, for example, has been practically redeemed within the last ten years. Many new tenements have been erected throughout this section, built, owned and tenanted by Italians. Fifteen years ago, before the Italian influx, 25 feet tenements were valued at from $10,000 to $15,000. They are now worth from $36,000 to $40,000. Adolfo Rossi states in his latest report to the Emigration Department of Italy that the character of Italian tenants and their prompt payments have lifted the valuation of tenement-house property in the Italian quarter to from $25,000 to $30,000, while like property in other quarters is valued at from $15,000 to $18,000.

There has been even a more notable change in the district running south of Washington Square to Canal Street and extending from Macdougal Street to West Broadway. Fifteen years ago this was one of the most notorious of the so-called slum quarters of the city, very largely tene-mented by negro and French families, and often glaring in its dissolute and riotous displays. Here the Italians began to settle about fourteen years ago, and their influx now dominates the section. Most of the French families have gone uptown, and few negroes are left, except in Third Street and Minetta Lane. Much of the property is held by old estates which have usually been backward in selling or improving. This disposition has retarded progress, but the advance of the section has nevertheless been remarkable. Now, whenever any real estate in this section comes into the market, it is eagerly bid for by Italian operators and builders. Hancock Street on both sides from Bleecker to Bedford now shows lines of tenements that would be a credit to any city. The popu-lation of this quarter is pre-eminently of Northern Italians —chiefly mechanics and storekeepers, earning unusually high average incomes, and naturally able to make the best showing of progress. The value of real estate in this section has greatly increased, and the quarter is, in the main, of excellent character.

Relatively less progress may be noted in other quarters, but there is no one in which a tenement occupied by Ital-ians is not regarded as an exceptionally profitable and certain investment. Italians are almost invariably prompt payers on rent day, and their landlords have no cause for worry over evasions and delays. The over-crowding by tenants is still too prevalent, and is wearing on the tenement quarters as well as detrimental to health, but in other respects Italian tenancy is distinctly desirable. No doubt, exhibits of filthy rooms may be brought to light, and the standard of personal cleanliness of recent immigrants from Southern Italy is undeniably low. But even the mass of these Italians like to have their homes neat and attractive, and Italian women as a body are excellent housewives.

Moreover, a growing improvement in these tenement-house districts is noted, as might be expected with the advance of greater permanency of settlement, and the disposition of Italians to invest their savings in real estate investments in the quarters where they live. The prevailing form of these investments is, of course, in tenement houses. The thrift of the Italian is so exceptional that even bootblacks and common laborers sometimes save enough to figure as tenement landlords. Italian barbers and grocery men quite frequently acquire equities in tenements. There is further a rising disposition of the more considerable merchants and especially of the fruiterers to invest their earnings in tenements in the Italian quarters.

Such investments, at first, are rarely sufficient to secure

clear title. The properties secured are usually heavily mortgaged. The small investor is likely to move into the house which he purchases and act as janitor and rent collector. If his calculations are correct, and he can keep his house full, he will pay off a considerable portion of the mortgage yearly, and in time become an unencumbered owner. Oftentimes a tenement is acquired too by obtaining a lease for from three to ten years before undertaking its purchase. If a favorable lease can be obtained, the saving by sub-letting may suffice to effect a purchase subsequently.

The increase of the real estate holdings thus acquired in New York is remarkable. It is stated by Mr. G. Tuoti, a representative Italian operator in real estate, that there was not a single Italian owner of real estate twenty years ago in the districts where the Italian owners now predominate. He has recently completed a list of more than eight hundred land owners of Italian descent in this city, whose aggregate holdings are approximately $15,000,000. This is the more noteworthy because the disposition of the Italians to invest in real estate here is of comparatively recent growth, and the common use of their savings has been to establish themselves in business.

A highly reliable computation of Italian savings and investments in New York City has lately been furnished by Mr. Gino C. Speranza, Vice-President of the Society for the Protection of Italian Immigrants. He reckons the individual holdings of Italians in the city savings banks to aggregate over $15,000,000. Their real estate holdings are said to approximate 4,000, of the clear value of $20,000,-000. He estimates that 10,000 stores in the city, speaking roundly, are owned by Italians, and sets their value at $7,000,000, to which may be added a further investment in wholesale business of about $7,000,000. The total material value of the property of the Italian colony in New York is over $60,000,000 by his computation, a value, as he states, relatively much below that of the Italian possessions in St. Louis, San Francisco, Boston and Chicago, but "a fair showing for the greatest 'dumping ground' of America."

The progress of the Italians in New York City is even more significantly shown by other summaries. The organization of the Italian Chamber of Commerce has been one of the most efficient agencies for the promotion of profitable trade between Italy and this country and the advance of Italian unity and enterprise. This chamber was founded in 1887 with only a few charter members, but now embraces over two hundred in its membership, comprising a majority of the principal Italian business men in greater New York. The advance of the Italian in the line of the professions in the city is shown by the reckoning of one hundred and fifteen Italian registered physicians, sixty-three pharmacists, four dentists, twenty-one lawyers, fifteen public school teachers, nine architects, four manufacturers of technical instruments and seven mechanical engineers.

There are over three hundred Italian "banks" so-called in the city, though probably nine-tenths of them are little more than remitting and transportation agencies. Some, however, are transacting a regular banking business and are of excellent standing. A very considerable number of the Italians are depositors in city savings banks, and there is one distinctively Italian savings bank on the corner of Mulberry and Spring Streets, which has an aggregate of deposits approximating $1,100,000, and 7,000 open accounts, roundly, showing an average of about $170 for each depositor. Two Italian steamship lines, with bi-weekly sailings from New York have been established in addition to the general foreign lines. Sixteen daily and weekly Italian newspapers in New York City alone show that Italians here have become newspaper readers more generally than in their own country.

Through the efforts of the missionary sisters of the Sacred Heart, and the contributions of resident Italians, the Columbus Hospital was founded in 1892, and is doing remarkably effective service in proportion to its available means. It is recognized as an Italian foundation distinctively, yet there is not the slightest prejudice of nationality in its conduct, as is apparent in the organization of its medical and surgical staff, for not one of its twenty-three physicians is an Italian. Another really admirable

foundation for charitable purposes is the Italian Benevolent Institute at 165–167 Houston Street, and contributors have the certain assurance that every dollar is
most prudently and fitly expended. The organization
for self or co-operative help is now widespread, and there
are over one hundred and fifty Italian Societies for mutual
aid and social improvement ends of one sort or another
in Manhattan alone.

The traditional eminence of Italy in art is maintained
in the choice of the late Italian Director of the Metro-
politan Museum of Art, and the certainty of the development of the Italian genius for art works is manifest in the
proficiency of Italian-American children in all primary
schools of drawing and design. Already the Italians of
New York have contributed three monuments to the city
and they are now raising funds to build a school in honor
of Verdi. The love of music is practically universal.
Almost all Italians have correct ears, if not trained voices,
and the humblest bootblack is more likely to mark flaws
in execution than the average opera-house goer. The
works of the favorite composers are familiar to the masses,
and the operas of Bellini, Donizetti, Verdi, Mascagni and
others never fail to draw large Italian audiences in New
York, if the leading singers are Italian.

In the smaller American cities of the Eastern States
the comparative advance and condition of the Italian
influx are commonly better in essential points than in New

York, Philadelphia and Boston. The foremost in these cities are not as wealthy as the leading Italian business men of New York, but the average living is more health-ful and desirable. There are rarely any big, dark tene-ments to invite congestion and disease. The lodging houses are often shabby and dingy, but they are quite commonly old residence houses with fairly spacious rooms, and the poorest are usually open to sunlight and fresh air. House and room rents are lower, and there is less pressure of applicants. There is still a tendency to over-crowding, but no approach to actual indecency. There are convenient places for the children to play without risking their lives and becoming a nuisance in congested streets. Social influences generally are more uplifting, and the children especially show the improvement.

All these points I have noted in close personal investi-gation in the cities of New England and the Middle States chiefly attracting Italian immigration. Bridgeport is one of the most progressive of the smaller cities on the Atlantic coast, and it assuredly makes a remarkable exhibit of the utilization and value of diversified immigration. A common prejudice against immigration springs from the assumption that it is filling the openings for employment here to the exclusion of American workmen. The actual effect—on the contrary—is marked in the development of Bridgeport. From the reckoning of the Board of Trade it appears that there are more expert mechanics in this

city than in any other in the State, and that the influx
of immigrants has operated to extend greatly the demand
for skilled labor, which is drawn from New England and
the Middle States. Thus the labor of American workmen
has not been displaced, but attracted.

It is estimated that the population of this city of Italian
descent is now approximately 3,500. In view of the fact
that the bulk of the Italian immigration has been of common laborers, doing the crudest and heaviest outdoor work
at the lowest wages of unskilled labor, their persistent
thrift and advance as a body are remarkable. There are
practically no drones nor beggars among them, and only
a small percentage is driven by sickness to the almshouse
or receives any support from charitable associations. It
is found, too, in Bridgeport, as elsewhere in New England,
that temporary help usually suffices to render applicants
self-supporting.

A considerable number of the working men have put
their savings into little shops, and in the extension of the
fruit business they have been notably successful—two of
them having become the leading dealers of the city. One
has founded and is successfully conducting a progressive
Italian newspaper, Il Sole, published semi-weekly, and
circulating widely beyond Bridgeport. They have organized a church society and recently dedicated a representative church, and their settlement is now firmly established. It is reckoned that they now own property in

the city to the extent of fully $800,000, and they have shown themselves heartily appreciative of the advantages and opportunities of American citizenship. They are law-abiding, remarkably temperate, devoted to their families and very anxious to give their children the advantage of the education that has not been open to them in the country of their birth. The Italian women are exemplary in their chastity and family relations.

The mayor of Bridgeport, the city clerk and representatives of leading savings banks have given special testimonials to the good character, industry, thrift and loyal American citizenship of the Italian settlement in Bridgeport. Mayor Mulvihill observed that: "The Italians are a religious and law-abiding people, and will compare favorably with any equal portion of American citizens whether native or adopted." City Clerk Buckingham stated: "There is no doubt that at the present time the standard of Italian citizenship is of a higher grade in this country than ever before, and what is true of the country in general is true of Bridgeport in particular. * * * To-day we find the Italian taking a prominent part in all the paths of life, in professions as well as in business. All professions are open to him, and to-day Bridgeport can point with pride to her bright and intelligent Italian doctors, lawyers, ministers and business men." The representatives of the leading savings banks report that the Italians are largely depositors, and that their deposits are steadily increasing. Their promptness in meeting obligations and their trustworthiness in general are particularly commended. The influx of Italian immigrants found employment at first chiefly in city and railway improvements. As their occupations became more varied and their familiarity with the conditions of living here advanced, their homes have been scattered throughout the city and their assimilation has been more rapid.

Throughout New York State the general reports were hardly less favorable. The mayors of Schenectady and Syracuse, among others called upon for information, were particularly emphatic in their certification of the service, progress and general good citizenship of the Italians in their cities.

Mayor Eisenmenger of Schenectady, which has been advancing industrially of late years more rapidly than any other city in the State, is strongly impressed by the working service and faculty of self support of the Italians. They are not disposed, he says, to jar with other nationalities, and the Italian is rarely the aggressor in any such dispute. They found employment originally chiefly in railway grading and city road work, but many are now small and apparently prospering tradesmen, and are acquiring homes of their own in and near the city. They appear to be almost uniformly anxious to urge the education of their children, and he has seen no reason to question their progressive assimilation.

The Italian in America

Mayor Alan C. Fobes of Syracuse considers that the Italians are of indispensable service in filling the demand for laborers for railway building and grading, and for state and city public works. He regards them as exceptionally reliable and persistent in their work when they are given employment, and believes that they constitute now an essential part of the working community in Syracuse. He would consider any move to displace them or discourage their coming by prejudiced legislation as decidedly unwise, and sees no reason to question the certain assimilation of their children, at least, in the American stock without any depreciation of its average quality.

Mr. Giles H. Stilwell, President of the Board of Education in Syracuse, substantially confirms the view of Mayor Fobes—writing in response to an inquiry—"We have quite a good many Italians and Austrians here, but they seem to be well disposed to work, are continually employed, and, instead of being a charge on the city, are generally, to all appearances, saving money, and many of them sending it back to the countries from which they came. There is no complaint here that they are not becoming Americanized."

In Utica the enterprising Italians have built an attractive theatre or opera house of their own. I was present one Saturday evening when nearly every seat was filled by an audience that was entertained by a performance of Monte Cristo. The performers were a well-balanced stock

86

company of eighteen members, uncommonly versatile artists, as the offer for the following Monday was the opera of Cavalleria Rusticana. The stage properties were nothing to brag of, but the acting was sympathetic and often vivid. The play was followed with a rapt attention that would greatly flatter American stock actors, but the Italians took the tribute of courtesy as a matter of course. This undertaking may not be a business success, for its Italian patrons are poor and there has been as yet no considerable attraction of American theatre-goers. But the enterprise is a signal evidence of Italian progress in America and of comparative refinement of taste, for ordinary vaudeville shows in this theatre and outside failed to attract Italian patronage. There is a childish gratification in the marionette shows in New York and other cities, but whenever an Italian theatre of any standing is opened, like the theatre Drammatico Nazionale of the Bowery or the new theatre in Utica, the plays that draw are plays of merit.

In the cities of the South and West the comparative prosperity of the Italians is even more pronounced, for the demand for their labor is keener than in more thickly settled communities.

There are between thirteen and fourteen thousand, according to the latest enumeration, in the Italian colony in New Orleans: 93 per cent. of them are Sicilians. Their industry and orderliness confute the prejudice which still lingers against the immigrants from the southern Italian provinces. Under fair conditions, as in this city, there are no widespread disturbances nor any ground for complaints against the mass of the townspeople. The leading business men are now planning to establish an Italian Chamber of Commerce, and it is probable that a labor bureau will be organized by this chamber to provide for meeting the great demand for labor coming from the interior of Louisiana, Florida, Alabama, Tennessee, Texas, Oklahoma and Indian Territory, for which region New Orleans is now the main centre of supply of Italian immigrant labor. An Italian foundation, especially commended by Signor Rossi after his recent inspection, is the Sacred Heart Mission which has established dependent elementary schools, a kindergarten and orphanage. In these schools, as Signor Rossi reports, thousands of Italian children learn Italian and English; many orphans of immigrants are fed, clothed, lodged and educated, and several hundred Italian immigrants yearly receive help of essential service.

The conditions in the smaller cities and towns are, as a rule, more favorable for the quick advance and independence of the immigrant colonists, for whom opportunities are open as artisans, small shopkeepers and cultivators of market gardens or outlying farms. There is no evidence in these communities of any aversion to agricultural occupations, for most of the new comers are eager to seek employment upon the suburban truck farms, and to undertake farming on the "half share" system, or by purchase of land when they are able to do so.

This is signally evident in the notable Italian colony at Bryan, Texas, which is of peculiar interest as an object lesson for the instruction and advantage of the mass of Italian immigrants to this country. Here a settlement of Sicilians, numbering about twenty-four hundred, has been prospering for several years. The families are spread over the neighborhood to a distance of eighteen miles from the town, and are, for the most part, proprietors of lands chiefly sown with Indian corn and cotton.

The families that rent lands generally pay $5.00 a year per acre, and it is reported by Signor Rossi that the families of the owners and tenants save from $100 to $1,000 yearly, according as they are more or less numerous and economical, and as the crops are more or less abundant. The greater part of these families came originally from Trapani in the neighborhood of Palermo, and in point of industry, thrift, good conduct and prosperity, they need not shun comparison with the immigrants from any other part of Italy or from any other country. Two years ago the parish priest of Bryan raised, in a few days, the contribution of $1,100 from his parishioners to pay for the construction of the local Catholic church, now ornamented with altar cloths embroidered in gold and other costly embellishments. All who came to greet Signor Rossi last year at the home of the parish priest gave evidence of their happy living and good prospects.

All the chief food supplies are here abundant and cheap, meat selling at five cents a pound. Taxation was said to be exceedingly light. The climate was judged to be fully as good as that of Sicily. There is much fertile land to be obtained for cultivation, and the owners give the use of the land without charge for two years to the farmer who clears it. The settlers cut down the trees, selling the wood at $2.00 per cord, and harvest Indian corn in the first year and cotton in the second.

In others of the small Texas towns the experience of Italian colonization in Bryan has been substantially duplicated, and the recent inspection of Signor Rossi has demonstrated that there is not a single city or town in Texas that has received immigration from Italy in which the newcomers are not as a body thrifty and comparatively well-to-do. The like is reported of the Italian settlers in Salt Lake City, and, after crossing the Sierras, the exhibit of Italian prosperity in the Californian cities and towns is still more noteworthy. Doubtless other parts of our country will prove as attractive to Italian immigration, and the opportunities for money making existing to-day in other sections may be even greater, as the most pressing demand for labor in this great Pacific coast state continues only for a part of the year, in the season of harvest; but Italian settlement in this state began with the earliest period of any considerable immigration, and the progress attained is naturally more pronounced and gratifying to the pride of the settlers.

In Los Angeles and the neighborhood there are now about four thousand Italians, chiefly coming to this country from Northern Italy, principally occupied as merchants and farmers, and Signor Rossi reports that all are industrious. "Not a few," he says," are rich owners of houses, farms and business properties."

The Italians in San Francisco are no less thrifty. In the neighborhood of the city there are about two hundred and fifty truck farms cultivated by Italian owners, chiefly Genoese, as Signor Rossi observes, "who obtain the manure from the stables in the city gratis and transform into fertile lands the original sand dunes." In this city also there is the noteworthy establishment of the California Fruit Growers' Association, in which are employed several hundred Italians, chiefly women, in the canning of asparagus, apricots and other vegetables and fruit. These employees work by the day, earning daily wages of from 75 cents to $2.00. The general superintendent of the association is an Italian, Signor Marco J. Fontana, "an interesting type of the self-made man," as Signor Rossi has lately remarked. There is, however, no desire on the part of the leading Italians of the city to induce any influx of immigration to seek employment within the city limits, as the organized labor unions practically control the trades and are jealous of any intrusion of non-union labor, and the directors of the Royal Italian Emigration Department advise the immigrants to avoid as far as practicable any conflict with American labor unions. Instead of promoting immigration in the face of such antagonism, as Signor Rossi shrewdly observes, "It is better to allow it to develop slowly and spontaneously, as it has up to the present time."

Outside of the famous vineyards, described in a following chapter, perhaps the most flourishing establishment of Italians in California is at San Jose, the principal centre of the fruit production of the Santa Clara valley. Here from three to four thousand Italians are profitably occupied as laborers, truck farmers and workers in the fruit-canning factories. In the beautiful valley surrounding the city not less than two hundred and fifty Italians are reported to be owners of small fruit farms.

The comparative progress and condition of the Italians in the American cities and towns in which openings for employment in market-gardening, fruit and vegetable handling and closely allied occupations are most abundant, clearly indicate the lines of advance to be preferred by Italian immigrants to this country.

ELIOT LORD.

CHAPTER V

The capacity of the Italian immigrant to make headway in this hustling country often against the keenest competition has been abundantly demonstrated. Unless he is grossly misplaced and handicapped, he will contrive to earn a living and save money with which to better his condition. Even the poorest and most dependent unskilled laborer saved some money, as a rule, in the early years of immigration when the labor conditions of this country were little known to the mass of Italians, and an immigrant was likely to come over under contract with some padrone.

If the padrone acted as a manufacturer's or contractor's agent, he would contrive to get commissions and other profits both from the buyer and the seller of labor at the expense of the immigrants, for all these exactions were deducted, in the long run, from the market rates for labor. If the padrone was only a greedy speculator, as was often the case, he would pay transportation expenses and as little more as he could possibly bargain for, and use or sell the labor in ways most profitable to himself.

The most outrageous impositions were through the securing of children as servitors of the padrone until this, as well as the contract labor practice, was squelched by the laws and the vigilance of prosecution.

Yet even under these intolerable exactions, the poorest immigrants continued to struggle along and reach independence sooner or later. Many of the most prospering and worthy Italian-American citizens to-day began their life in this country as bootblacks, newsboys or strolling musicians in the grip of padrones. This distressful experience is no longer imposed—or, if continued, the violation of law is covert and rare. The padrone now survives only in the tolerable form of an employment agent and boarding-house keeper, and his chances of profit are vanishing yearly with the increasing information and self-reliance of the immigrant as the numbers of his countrymen increase in this country.

There can be no possible question that the average condition and earnings of the common unskilled Italian laborer are materially better in this country to-day than they were twenty years ago. This advance is due to his better guidance and equipment for competition, and it is practically certain that the market value of his labor will continue to rise with the rising appreciation of his capacity and the growing reluctance of competing laborers to do the crudest, most fatiguing and least profitable work. In view of his present employment in road making, railway grading, track laying, cargo handling and other public and private works, it is not likely that he has any competition to fear.

In more advanced industrial employment his competing capacity is no less evident. In some occupations it has been strained to excess through his eagerness to earn money, or under the pressure of actual want. It may be unfortunate for him if the anticipation of the Industrial Commission of 1901 is realized, "that the future clothing workers of the country are not likely to be the Jews but the Italians." Yet it is certainly remarkable that the Italian peasants who come to this country so soon learn to turn their hands to the making of clothing and other manufactures in which they have had no prior experience. The number of immigrants formally entered as "tailors" is assuredly very much less than the number engaged in the making of clothing in our American cities.

This facility is explained in the report of the Industrial Commission, no doubt correctly. "The Italian, like the Jew, has a very elastic character. He can easily change habits and modes of work and adapt himself to different conditions; he is energetic and thrifty, and will work hard with little regard for the number of hours. It is quite usual for an Italian cloak-maker, like the Jew, after he has worked 10 hours in the shops with his wife, to take a bundle of work home at night. But, unlike the Jew, he not only does the work at home himself, but he is assisted by the women in his family, and often leaves a part of the work for them to do during the day."

"If the Italian and the Pole are compared, it will be found that it is the Polish women who enter the sewing trade, whereas the former Polish farmer clings to common work requiring hard labor. The Italian is able on account of his national characteristics, artistic ability, etc., to control such work as the manufacture of clothing, silk weaving, hat making and other trades where taste and a fine sense of touch are essential for a successful performance of the work. The Polish farmer can successfully compete in factory work where hard automatic labor is necessary; but the Italian dislikes mechanical work and is better adapted to diversified pursuits where manipulation is required."

"Notwithstanding the competing power of Polish women" (due to their unequalled endurance), "they can probably be excelled by Italian women. While a great many Polish women have entered the trade, they have not yet developed great speed nor been able to work in factories producing the best grades of work, while Italian women are almost perfect imitators. The Italian women can develop speed and can work with skill. Like the Poles, they also are obedient to orders."

In the record of the distribution of Italian immigrants by trades and industries for the fiscal year ending June 30, 1903, it is noteworthy that the immigrant masons outnumber the artisans attached to any other single industry or trade. 4,226 entered in this year, and the allied branch of stonecutters contributed an additional 978. This is a significant exhibit of the demand in this country for workers in occupations in which the Italian is an acknowledged expert. It is unquestionable that there would be a much greater influx of these valuable artisans, if available openings for employment were better determined and reported, and if the antagonism of the labor unions to any outside competition was not so pronounced. Expertness in quarrying and stone cutting, as well as in plastering and moulding, has been a transmitted acquirement for more than two thousand years in Italy, and the skilled Italian workman in these lines of industry, ascending to the pinnacle of the fine arts of sculpture and cameo cutting, dreads no competition. This influx is not now artificially stimulated in any way through the agency of contractors, and its distribution is now so widespread and scattering that it does not appear to arouse any special antagonism.

Immigrant barbers and hair-dressers come next to the masons in numbers according to the same year's record, showing a total of 4,145. Their competence and conduct are certainly not below the average in this country as the multiplication of their shops bears witness, even in quarters where there are few if any Italian customers. Tailors stand third in the same list, numbering 3,464, and carpenters and joiners make a close fourth with a total of 2,979. Italian cabinet makers, picture-frame joiners and gilders and other artistic wood workers are often very deft, and the average workman is likely to hold his own in any ordinary competition.

It is interesting to note a contribution in this single year of 146 "sculptors and artists" and 305 "musicians," showing that the fine arts in this country are absorbing an increasing supply of Italian talent or genius. The handiwork of naturalized Italians as well as of their children born in this country may be seen in pictures and statuary and mural decorations adorning many fine residences in America. Although the great mass of the immigrants has been made up of the poor, ill-educated, cafoni and farm laborers, it is noteworthy how surely the innate artistic powers of this stock come to light and expand in the attainments of their children under the culturing influences of our schools of design.

The professional and business men who have come to this country from Italy and those who have been reared here of Italian parentage are not, as yet, sufficient in number to make any considerable collective impress, except in a few cities like New York and San Francisco, but their talents and character and the innate courtesy that marks their people from peasant to sovereign have already won deserved recognition and cordial acceptance for them as a fine type of Americans.   John J. D. Trenor.

CHAPTER VI

IN THE MINING FIELDS

The number of Italian immigrants giving their occupation as miners, as reported in the official returns, is by no means an accurate gauge of the influx into our mining fields, for the greater part of the workers in the coal fields, at least, are not trained miners, but are drawn from the ranks of common laborers who are employed in surface work of the simplest kinds, where their lack of experience is not a final disqualification.

The record of the entry of Italian "miners," however, shows clearly enough the beginning of any considerable intrusion into our coal-mining fields. From 1875 to 1880 inclusive the average yearly entry of Italian immigrant miners was only 37. In 1881 this average was nearly quadrupled, and in the following year the number entering was nearly ten times the former average. This influx continued during the next ten years without materially increasing the record of 1882 except in 1889, when the unprecedented number of 767 is recorded. In the closing years of the decade ending with 1900 the average rose materially, the influx reaching 863 in 1899 and 1,260 in

1900.   Three years later the record for the year was 2,520, showing a still more noteworthy increase.   By far the greater part of this immigration came from Northern Italy to our mining fields, the proportion in 1899 being more than 7 to 1 from Southern Italy, and in 1900 being almost exactly like that of the previous year.

Presumably most of the immigrants recording themselves as miners have had some previous training, at least, in mining work at home, and the fact will not be disputed that many Italians included in the record lists are expert operators, but, as before noted, these workmen constitute only a fraction of the number seeking employment in the coal fields.

Such employment, especially in the anthracite fields, has been one of the least desirable and satisfactory occupations of the Italian in this country.   Mining is arduous and dangerous at best, and it has been prosecuted in our coal fields under lax mining laws, hampered and unsound administration and labor conditions often intolerable.   The entry of the Italians into the mining fields of this country corresponded closely with the introduction of machines for coal mining.

In the words of the Report of the Illinois Bureau of Labor Statistics for 1888: "A mining machine not only reverses the customary methods of work but changes equally the system of wages.   The coal miner proper was accustomed to take his own tools into the pit and to deliver from the wall of mineral before him certain tons of coal ready every morning for a certain sum per ton. He mined, drilled, blasted and loaded his own coal, timbered his own roof, took care of his own tools, and was responsible mainly to himself for his personal safety in the amount of his output.''

''In the machine mine some seven or eight men are required to perform these functions. In the mine, as in the mill, the machine has become the master and the men are its servitors. The operator and the mechanism simply direct its energies when the motive power is given to it, and the coal is under cut or mined. A blaster follows with tools and explosives, loosening the mass; the loaders reduce it and shovel it into pit cars; the timber men follow and prop the roof which no longer has the mineral to rest upon. Labor is assisted in every process and a machinist is retained for repairs. Each one does his own certain portion of the work and no more, and doubtless does it better as well as faster by reason of the greater skill thus acquired. Herein lies the chief value of the machine to the mine owner. It relieves him for the most part of skilled labor and of all the restraint which that implies. It opens to him the whole labor market from which to recruit his force; it enables him to concentrate the work of the mine at given points, and it admits of the graduation of wages to specific work and of the payment of wages by the day.''

" The results of this introduction of machinery consist not only in the greater execution of the machine, but in the subdivision of labor which it involves, and the greater per capita efficiency of the force thus secured. The gain is consequently to the employer rather than to the men. The mining machine is, in fact, the natural enemy of the coal-miner: it destroys the value of his skill and experience, obliterates his trade, and reduces him to the rank of a common laborer or machine driver if he remains where he is."

Statistics taken from average mining establishments show that the expert cutters and blasters who take the places of the miners in a hand mine—not exceeding eight per cent. of the total number employed in a machine mine —receive higher wages per day than the miners displaced. It is reckoned that this increase amounts to an advance of about 22% in wages, but the certain immediate effect of the introduction of machines in mining is to reduce very greatly the number of skilled miners formerly employed, displacing, on the average, 60% of the total number formerly engaged in the hand mines.

It is commonly reckoned that the entry of the workers from Southern Europe into our coal-mining fields displaced a very large proportion of the former workers, who were almost all English-speaking miners. Examination of the records shows that this conclusion is not fully justified. There is only a very trivial difference in num-

In the Mining Fields

bers, for example, between the foreign-born English-speaking miners employed in the entire anthracite coal region in 1900 and the force employed in 1880 before the advent of the mass of the immigrants from Southern Europe engaged in coal mining. But it is undoubtedly true that the natural increase in the number of the foreign-born English-speaking miners has been almost completely checked, and an actual loss in numbers is shown if the record of 1890 is compared with that of the later year, 1900. Of the new elements which have entered this coal field and forestalled the increase of the English-speaking miners, the Lithuanians, Slovaks and Poles constitute by far the greater part.

The number of Italians in the entire anthracite region of Pennsylvania in 1900—Carbon, Columbia, Dauphin, Lackawanna, Luzerne, Northumberland, Schuylkill and Susquehanna counties—is reckoned by Frank Julian Warne ("The Slav Invasion," p. 51) at only 9,958, or hardly more than one-twentieth of the total foreign born in this region, so that the Italian immigrant, at least, can scarcely be charged with any considerable responsibility for the depression of the standard of living in that section at large.

One main objection to the opening afforded for the employment of Italians in these fields is that it has drawn very little comparatively from the number of skilled miners, possibly available in Italy, by far the larger proportion being made up of the ordinary unskilled laborers employed in surface work as helpers and slate pickers. This crude employment is particularly disadvantageous in that it opens no considerable prospect of progress and no training in the expert branches of mining for which relatively high pay is conceded. The experts in the mines have contrived to guard their positions strictly and jealously through the organization of miners' unions limiting the numbers of those available for service, and requiring long terms of apprenticeship. Moreover, the work in these fields for most employees has been more or less uncertain and irregular, continuing for a limited part of the year only, and enforcing periods of idleness and consequent waste of earnings.

It is further notable that the percentage of accidents among the inexperienced Italian laborers thus employed is exceptionally high, although they are not engaged, as a rule, in the most dangerous tasks of underground mining. The Slavs have been notoriously reckless, but the Italians do not appear to be chargeable with any lack of precaution except the imprudence necessarily resulting from their ignorance of the attendant risks. Yet in spite of a general caution, which has been sneeringly charged to them as evidence of timidity, it is unquestionably the fact that the Italian laborers have suffered as much as any, proportionately, from accidents in the fields.

There is further a noted jealousy on the part of the other miners, holding aloof as a body from the more recent immigrants, and practically constraining the Italians as well as the Slavs to cluster together in settlements exceedingly unfavorable to their assimilation and progress. It is unfortunately true also that there has been an apparent jangling and bitterness between the Slavs and Italians themselves, as well as among the different divisions of the Slavic and other races that have entered the fields. This dissension has been overcome in large measure of late years through the length of association in the fields, and particularly by the efforts of the intelligent directors of the American Federation of Labor to promote a better concord and co-operation for the common protection and advancement. Nevertheless, during the twenty years closing the last century, during which the influx of immigration from Southern Europe first began and continued in increasing numbers, the social condition of these immigrants in the fields has been little short of deplorable.

As the Italians have been relatively inconsiderable in number, they have escaped the brunt of the antagonism which has been directed against the influx from Austria-Hungary and Russia, termed by a recent writer, Frank Julian Warne, "The Slav Invasion." The Slavs have been accused of flocking in recklessly, regardless of any existing standard of wages or effort for its maintenance and accepting any rate of pay which would enable them to earn the barest livelihood. As so large a proportion of them have been unmarried men, and their standard of living has been so low compared with that maintained and demanded by the English speaking miners, there can be no question that the competition thus enforced has been exceedingly severe and detrimental to the average social condition of the mass of workmen in the mining fields.

It was to be expected, however, that the introduction of machines, with its inevitable decrease of the number of experts required for mine operation, would tend at the outset inevitably to the lowering of wages and social conditions. This tendency has been offset in a measure through the general prosperity and progress of the country, greatly extending the demand for the coal product of the fields, and thereby extending the demand for labor employed in production. It is certain that the advance due to this economic condition has already been material, and the rate of wages has further been maintained and advanced through the labor union organizations arraying themselves in opposition to the pressure of capital seeking the cheapest labor in the market and enforcing the allowance of better pay, more just regulations and shorter hours for the employees. At the present time it is unquestionable that the condition of the laborers in the mining fields of Pennsylvania, West Virginia and other states east of the Mississippi has been very materially bettered through their perfected organization and the extraordinary industrial progress of the country at large. There is relief, too, from the growing disposition of the sons of the miners to

In the Mining Fields

enter other occupations. The "brightest Irish boys in the anthracite coal fields," wrote an experienced observer in "The Outlook," August 5, 1899, "one of the operators told me, do not work in the mines, but go on the railroads or into stores or teach school." Yet, at best, the prospects open for Italian labor in these fields are hazardous and relatively undesirable, and the mass of Italians at least should be persistently advised to seek for employment along more profitable lines, for which they are far better adapted by natural taste and former training.

In the mining fields west of the Mississippi the labor and social conditions have commonly been much more satisfactory, and the openings for the extension of Italian labor are undoubtedly far more promising. This has lately been shown authoritatively in the report of the visiting inspector of the Royal Immigration Department, Signor Rossi. The reported conditions in Indian Territory, to which many Italian miners as well as farm workers have been strongly attracted in recent years, are without exception favorable for contented and prosperous Italian employment.

According to figures furnished by leading residents, the number of Italians, including women and children now living in the mining fields in Indian Territory, is as follows:

In McAlister	200
In Krebs	2,000
In Colgate	1,500
In Philips	500
In Archibald	30
In Alderson	500
In Hartshorne	400
Other localities...............................	500

South McAlister is particularly noted in the inspector's report as a small city of about 7,000 inhabitants that has developed with wonderful rapidity, thanks to the new and rich coal mines recently discovered in the neighborhood. The richest and most intelligent Italians located here are said to be the Fassino Brothers, the Piedmontese proprietors of a macaroni factory and of a carriage and wagon warehouse. One of the brothers informed the inspector that many Italian miners had come into the territory within the last few years since the discovery of new coal mines and that all were doing very well. The opportunity to acquire land was commonly very attracttive. The price ranged from two and three to fifteen dollars per acre. Signor Fassino told the inspector that he had already invested sixty thousand dollars in land, and that, if he had more money to spare, he would buy still more, being certain that in three years he would triple his capital. The Fassino Brothers were at the start miners. They engaged in business as soon as they had saved some money, and had been residing in the territory for many years and assisting in the development of the country.

In the Mining Fields

About two hundred Piedmontese miners were living at McAlister in small wooden houses. They told the inspector that they earned " very good wages," $2.56 for a day of eight hours, and many at the mines were doing piece work by preference. Their only complaint was the prohibition against alcoholic drinks. The Piedmontese told the inspector that the work in the mines was necessarily fatiguing, and that they were obliged frequently to labor in very hot galleries where the air was vitiated by the gas coming from the coal seams. When they went out at night they "needed something to drink stronger than water in order to catch their breath." One miner said: "I worked for years in Asia Minor; notwithstanding that the Koran strictly forbids to Mohammedans the use of spirituous drinks, the Turks allowed us Christians to drink wine, beer and other liquors at our pleasure." Signor Rossi notes as a curious circumstance in view of the prohibition of the use of any kind of alcoholic drinks in the Territory that Fernet is admitted as a febrifuge and that a large amount of this liquor is consumed.

At Krebs the inspector found about two thousand Italians working, also largely Piedmontese. On account of the temporary restriction of business in the year of the Presidential Election, the miners here did not have work for the entire week, "but, nevertheless, if they worked four or five days out of the six, the miners did well, because almost all do piece work, and there are those who earn

The Italian in America

$80 every two weeks. 'I will wager,' said a well-known fellow of the place, 'that here at Krebs there are at least fifty thousand dollars buried under ground; the workmen are justly afraid of the so-called bankers and prefer to hide their money.'" In a general store in the town the inspector saw affixed to the wall a list of seven thousand francs that an Italian priest had collected for the construction of a new church at Castigleone di Carovilli. This money was contributed by the immigrants from that place who are working at Krebs, at Brookside in Colorado and at Hubbard in Ohio. The best store in Krebs was kept by a Sicilian from Sciacca. Seeing that this store was prospering, some six or seven other Italian stores were opened, a little too many, the inspector thought, for Krebs.

Some of the miners cultivated vegetables in the garden patches, enclosing their little wooden houses, but this diversion was not common, for the miners generally had no inclination for farming nor even for truck gardening. This is regretted by the inspector, who regards the Indian Territory as one of the sections in North America that should be taken into serious consideration by those in search of land for cultivation. In its valleys every product of the temperate zone may be raised readily, and on the hills vines will surely flourish, as a successful experiment by an Italian has already proved.

At Thurber in Texas, Signor Rossi visited the five well-developed coal mines of the Texas and Pacific Coal Company in which about eight hundred miners of various nationalities were at work. More than one-third of these were Italians. The local Italian colony here numbers about five hundred, including the women and children. It has a school and Catholic church in charge of a Sicilian priest. Its workmen are for the greater part Venetians, Piedmontese and Modenese.

Thurber has now about five thousand inhabitants, and is a large village of neat wooden houses standing among green hills. All the land for many miles around was said to be the property of the Texas and Pacific Coal Company, which also owned the houses and stores. In spite of this monopoly the inspector noted that everything needed by the miners was sold at reasonable prices. The director of the mines, Mr. Gordon, told him that the Italians were the best workmen in his employ, and that the company was about to open new mines and had urgent need of hands. He stated that there was coal enough in the lands of the company to provide work for the next hundred years, and that his company was ready to make any reasonable provision to insure the attraction and continuance of Italian labor. "The colony of Thurber," continues the inspector, "is as industrious and tranquil as anyone could desire. There are very few disturbances, as is evident from the fact that there is only one policeman in the town, who is able to maintain order throughout the town as well as in the surrounding country."

The mines are located from three to six miles from the village, but in the morning and evening the miners are taken to work and back to their homes by two special trains. It was stated by the Italian workers at Thurber that the mining was hard because the stratum of coal was thin and the galleries therefore low, so that it was necessary to work in a crouching position; but, on the other hand, there was assurance of safety from the fact that the coal did not give off gas and that the galleries were perfectly dry. In consequence of the intervention of the United Mine Workers of America, it was said that from the 1st of October of the year, 1903, the working day had been reduced to eight hours and the pay increased to $1.17 1/2 per ton. A delegate of the union now assists at the weighing of coal in every mine. All the miners work by the piece, and according to their greater or lesser ability are earning from $2.50 to $3.00 and sometimes more per day. The pay for the other operators, blacksmiths, drivers, etc., is $2.40 per day. Inexperienced workers, on arrival, who begin as apprentices, earn at the start 1.00 per day, but in a few weeks they are said to learn the work and their wages increase week by week.

The inspector notes that the needed food supplies, bread, meat, fish, etc., are cheap. The unmarried miners are accustomed to live in boarding houses with families either of relatives or fellow-countrymen, paying for board $16.00 per month. The greater part, he reports, make notable savings; very few indeed spend all their 'wages.

The condition of the miners in Colorado the inspector found to be much less satisfactory, chiefly owing, however, to the long protracted strike. There were complaints also of monopolies and petty extortions, and at the time of his visit the demands of the miners' unions had not been enforced as thoroughly as in other states of the Central West and South.

JOHN J. D. TRENOR.

CHAPTER VII

ON FARM AND PLANTATION

Why have so few Italian immigrants, comparatively speaking, sought a livelihood and homes for themselves in our agricultural states and districts? The question is commonly asked in wonderment and often in reproach by those who see the Italian peasants clustering so persistently in our cities, although their former occupations and experience have been almost wholly confined to the tilling of the land and grape or olive growing. This apparent preference seems unaccountable to those who are not exactly informed in regard to the burdensome conditions under which the Italian peasant has been laboring in his own country, and the practical necessities confronting him when he lands in this country. A characteristic expression of this feeling appeared lately in the columns of one of the most judicious and sympathetic of American newspapers, the "New York Evening Post."

"What use has the New World made of the Italian? The greatest disappointment is from the industrial standpoint. With the blood of generations of peasants in his veins, the Italian here flocks by the hundreds of thou-

114

sands into the cities, and neglects the great farming countries of the South and West." This condition was largely
attributable, in the editor's view, to the childlike and dependent nature of the Italian, and the controlling influence
of the padroni who have profited by his ignorance and
helplessness, and "have reduced him almost to a state
of peonage." In spite of the laudable efforts noted of
the Italian Protective Society to better the situation, the
apparently gloomy conclusion was reached that "in the
main the American Italian has become a confirmed tenement dweller."

My inquiry now calls up the obverse point of view.
Instead of charging the Italian with neglecting the great
farming countries of the South and West, would it not be
more correct to urge that they have neglected him? What
have any of the Western or Southern States done, except
California and Louisiana, to attract or promote Italian
immigration and settlement? What has the body of
farmers and plantation owners done to open employment
on any practicable terms to the Italians? The Western
farming lands were very largely taken up in advance by
immigrants from Northern Europe before the advent of
the Italians in any considerable numbers here. The days
when accessible lands could be readily obtained under
our homestead laws were past. Preference was naturally
given by the Western settlers in possession to immigrant
helpers of their own nationalities, and opportunities for

securing land have been practically reserved for these affiliated colonists alone.

The Italian peasant or farm hand was of unknown and unproved value to the mass of employers in the West. A current depreciation of his character and service had prejudiced them against him, even when there was an opening for his labor which was not eagerly grasped by their own countrymen on the spot. They have had no active sentimental concern for the condition of the Italian peasant in our cities, and it is a very rare exception when any one of them has extended to him a helping hand or the offer of employment. Probably the greater part of them would declare to-day in ignorance or prejudice that they didn't want to make trial of Italian labor or to attract Italians to their districts. Even state officials and the working heads of land and immigration associations have been avowedly controlled by this prejudice in the discrimination of their invitations to settlers, and its existence in the Southern States has perhaps been even more strongly marked than in the West.

A notable instance in point to this effect is furnished by Mr. F. B. Gordon in his recent address as President of the Georgia Industrial Association. In urging the necessity of promoting white immigration, both native and foreign, to the Southern States, he called attention sharply also to the patent desirability of a more liberal spirit in the welcome to immigrants, and particularly with reference to the Italians. To illustrate the height of prevailing prejudice he cited the remarkable provision of a law of the State of South Carolina restricting immigration "to white citizens of the United States, citizens of Ireland, Scotland, Switzerland, France, and all other foreigners of Saxon origin." Both in published reports and in response to hundreds of inquiries directly addressed to immigration societies and land owners throughout the South, a very marked preference was shown for the attraction of native-born Americans already settled in the North and West rather than for the incoming of alien immigrants. This preference is largely due, of course, to the greater capital in money, goods and tools brought into the South by native settlers, and the fact that the openings for the men with some capital are much better assured at present than the steady employment of labor without capital to entrench it. Yet the more enlightened policy now fast extending through the South, as careful inquiries prove, is a hopeful assurance of the opening of greater opportunities in future years for the profitable employment of immigrants honestly seeking work and homes in this country.

In the light of all the facts in the case, too, the desponding conclusion that "the American Italian has become a confirmed tenement dweller" does not as yet appear to be justified. I have reached this conclusion not only from direct inquiries, but from the confirming observations of such expert investigators as Alessandro Mastro-Valerio of Chicago, editor of " La Tribuna Italiana," who has been notably successful in promoting the planting of Italian agricultural colonies here. In his discussion of the distribution of Italian immigration, embodied in the report of the Industrial Commission (Vol. XV, 1901), he has pointed out with undeniable force the depressing experience of the Italian peasant at home and the controlling reasons why his work has hitherto been confined so largely to our cities and railway lines. The Italian peasant, he writes, " has been kept in such subjection on account of his former occupation—agriculture—that he feels ashamed of himself and his work. He comes to this country still detesting it, and here he throws it away with the same pleasure that Hercules had in tearing from his body the shirt of Nessus."

He is further " entirely ignorant of the possibilities of American agriculture, and it never occurs to him that he could earn money and make a position for himself by tilling the American soil, having been accustomed to look with distrust and hate at the soil, not as the alma parens, but as a cruel and ungrateful stepmother. None of his countrymen who are already here and who send money home, or have brought it home themselves, ever write or say that they earn their money by working the soil, first for others, and afterwards for themselves, as farmers. Of the moral and material advantages of American coun-

try life, of the comfort and independence it affords, of
the rights and duties of the American farmer, as a pioneer
of civilization and as an exponent and example of the
American principles of self-government, which cannot be
learned in American cities, owing to political corruption,
he is totally ignorant, since he has always been a servant
of the glebe, with many duties to perform and very few
rights to enjoy."

Moreover, the greater part of the laborers who make
up the bulk of the immigration from Central and Southern
Italy, as pointed out in a former chapter, are not country-
folk, like the mass of American farm hands, but cafoni,
who have been dwellers in towns for centuries for needed
defence and security. They are accustomed to the society
of their own countrymen, and would naturally shrink
from isolation, particularly in a place where they are
ignorant of the language and customs and have no reason
to expect peculiar consideration or a disposition to put
up with shortcomings until they had grown familiar with
the requirements of employers. If they happened to
have wives or families with them, this shrinking would
be accented, for the Italian women are even more dependent on the society of neighbors for contented living than
their husbands would be. Above all comes, too, the
pressing necessity in their poverty of taking the first job
which comes to hand with the certainty of support. As
before noted, the first work offered to them on landing

on our seacoast is commonly not on a farm, but on docks
or railways or as a day laborer in or near American
cities.

Yet in spite of these obstacles to distribution, there is
no reason for discouragement if the character and habits
and training of the Italian are intelligently kept in view
and the lines of least resistance are followed.   The Italian
tenement-house population in New York City is constantly
shifting, year by year.   The Italians are growing keen
in their search for better quarters, and only cling to a
rookery till they see a chance to better their housing on
terms which they can afford to pay.   There is no exceptional difficulty in drawing an Italian and his family away
from New York if he sees a substantial prospect of bet-
tering his condition.   In the lesser cities of the state and
country there are comparatively few tenements in the
restricted sense in which the term is applied in New York
City.   In the other cities and towns where the immigrants
are clustering, they are living commonly in the older
residence houses, and often in those of comparatively good
class originally, which have been opened to tenants by a
shifting of their residents to outlying wards or sections.
These houses are often dilapidated and glaringly in want
of paint and repair, but they are not big congested rook-
eries, and even the poorest are commonly open to the air
and sunlight, and with a decent provision, at least, to meet
sanitary requirements.   There is no inevitable pressure to

degeneration and disease in such quarters, and if many
of the rooms appear ill-kempt and dirty in the American
eye, the filth of the quarters is rarely so great as to seriously threaten the health of the occupants or of the city
at large.

The readiest and easiest opening for the successful employment of the Italians on the land in this country and
the betterment of their distribution is offered in the extension of market gardening near our cities and towns.
In the care and perfecting of vegetable and small fruit
crops a great number of the immigrant peasants are already
adepts. The facility and success with which they are
taking up the occupations of fruit and vegetable handling
and selling in so many American cities to-day point
directly to the probability of an equal measure of success
in the growing and marketing of these products. Moreover, this is no longer simply a probable assumption. No
more successful instances of market gardening are apparent anywhere in this country than can be seen on the
land now cultivated by Italians. The Italian family is
peculiarly qualified to make headway in intensive farming, for the women and children take readily to the work
as well as the men, and contribute an often essential part
of the labor required for the support of the family and the
maturing of the crops.

Six years ago I was invited by one of the leading hotel
and restaurant keepers in New Haven to drive out with

him to look over a market garden which had been planted by a poor Italian and his family only a few years before near the suburbs of the city. I have never seen anywhere in this country a more thriving garden, nor one in which every possible means of advancing the crops that were available to a poor man had been more keenly noticed and grasped. The owner had even then made an unqualified success of his venture. He had largely extended his original holdings, was employing a number of his own countrymen as helpers, and delivering his produce in his own handsome market vans to shipping depots and an extended range of customers in the city, including all the principal hotels and restaurants. His garden beds were thoroughly cleaned of weeds and stones, and all highly fertilized by the systematic collection of street droppings and the addition of other manures. His laborers and children had diligently collected slightly broken and refuse window glass from all parts of the city, and he had used this glass at first exclusively in covering his plants to force their spring growth, though he was later able to replace these covers with neatly constructed forcing cases and greenhouses. Even with his rude appliances at the start he was able to market his vegetables in New Haven nearly two weeks earlier than the average of his neighbors and to reap the profits of a stinted supply and unsatisfied demand.

This same gardener has now a widely extended and

most thrifty plantation, giving employment in the season to 200 of his poorer countrymen, women and children, and holding up an object lesson by which many thousands of immigrants to this country should profit. It is very short-sighted fault-finding that would complain of this progress, as a New Haven clergyman did, because the laborers under him are earning as yet small wages, and are not housed commodiously. He is hiring his labor in the open market, as all other American employers do when they can, and his working people are glad of the opportunity offered to earn a certain and congenial living with the prospect of advancement on their own account independently, sooner or later.

The opportunities grasped by this Italian have not been exceptional. There is not a single one of the cities of this country yet reached by the Italians where there is available market land near by that is not now receiving vegetables and fruits as the produce of Italian labor. In fact, the employment of Italians in market gardening in our Northern States, on the Pacific coast and to some extent in the South, has been advancing of recent years with certain success and the most hopeful prospect. There is a really large sprinkling of them now profitably at work on Long Island and Staten Island, in the State of New Jersey, in the Delaware peach belt, in the large truck farming districts of Norfolk, Virginia, in the suburbs of Washington and Baltimore, and in many of the cities and towns of Massachusetts, Connecticut, Rhode Island, Pennsylvania and New York.

On the outskirts of Memphis, Tennessee, a large colony of Italian truck farmers is of particular note. These colonists all come from the neighborhood of the town of Alessandria, and their settlement is formally known from their pride in their birthplace as " La Colonia Alessandrina di Memphis." They have been successfully established for years in their pursuit of furnishing Memphis with fruit and vegetables, and are reported to be without exception well-to-do. This unbroken success is doubtless due largely to their neighborly affiliation and disposition to help one another. Certain assurance of co-operation and maintenance is marked in their organization of a mutual help society known as " La Societa di Muttuo Soccorso dei Giardinieri Italiani di Memphis," a provision which might be readily copied to advantage by their fellow-countrymen here and which is, indeed, now paralleled on a more restricted scale by the Italian sick, death and accident benefit societies already fast multiplying among the Italians in American cities. In his recent report to the Royal Emigration Department, the visiting inspector, Signor Rossi, made particular note of " the most beautiful truck farms " of this colony, and ascertained from the Italian Consular Agent at Memphis that the Italians in the State of Tennessee were approximately three thousand in number, "almost all farmers who were doing well."

On Farm and Plantation

Further south the truck farming settlements of Italians near New Orleans and Galveston are almost equally notable, and their success is an object lesson for the possible supply of many another Southern city—a lesson already appreciated by Dallas, Houston, San Antonio, and the larger Texan towns in whose suburbs Italian truck farming is already progressing successfully.

One of the most noteworthy instances of the feasibility of establishing this Italian immigrant industry on a basis entirely satisfactory is afforded by the plantations in the township of Canastota, N. Y. Here the Italians were first attracted by the offer of arable land to be worked on the share system, closely correspondent to the Tuscan mezzeria with which all natives of Central Italy are familiar. The land was divided into tracts, each assigned to a separate family. The needed seed or plants or tools for cultivation were furnished by the owners when required. A plain, small, but sufficient house was provided for each family, and the requisite credit for the food supply for the first season's work was extended.

Each cultivator had, as a rule, from five to six acres to care for. Here he produced onions, beets, spinach, cabbage, celery and other vegetables for which the demand was certain and the market ready. At the close of the season half the product was credited to him and half to his landlord, deducting advances for rent from the laborer's share of profits.

The Italian in America

The success of this undertaking was so marked from the start that its extension followed as a matter of course without any artificial urging. The number of Italians employed on these plantations has grown to over five hundred, including the women and children, as estimated by Hon. Milton Delano, President of the State Bank of Canastota. When I visited this township recently the permanence of this settlement was assured beyond question. Most of the Italians on the plantations had already saved enough to buy and own without debt their own little houses and farms, and some had considerably increased the size of their original holdings. All without known exception, as Mr. Delano reported, were thriving and contented. A considerable number had opened accounts in his bank, and many more were depositors in the savings banks of Syracuse and other neighboring cities.

There was no criminal disposition noted and there had never been any serious trouble in the settlement. The parents were ambitious for their children, and the children were eager to learn and would compare favorably with any other American children of the same age and condition in life. Mr. Delano and other well-informed American residents were unhesitating in their declaration that the character of the settlement was in all respects unexceptionable. It was particularly noted that the settlers were unusually prompt in paying their debts and meeting any obligations. Not one among them, Mr. Delano said, had ever been committed to the poorhouse or become a vagrant or called upon anybody for charitable relief. They had organized two benefit societies of their own, as a provision for sickness, accidental injury or death, and these associations were strong enough to respond to any call upon them. It is in such model settlements, the feasibility of whose extension is unquestionable, that one certain solution is presented of the so-called problem of Italian immigration.

In the cultivation of berries of every kind the Italian in America soon becomes particularly adept, even if he has had little previous training. This is so well attested that a single illustration may suffice, the advance of strawberry culture at Independence, Louisiana, since the entry of the Italian gardeners. Fifteen years ago there was not an Italian family in this settlement on the main line of the Illinois Central Railroad, sixty-two miles north of New Orleans. Now there are at least one hundred and sixty thriving Italian families in the township, and their work has made Independence the " blue ribbon " strawberry shipper of Louisiana, if not of the country at large.

The railroad and bank reports for the season of 1904 credit the berry growers and pickers of Independence with the shipment of two hundred and seventy-five carloads of berries of unsurpassed quality to St. Louis, Chicago, Cincinnati and the Southern markets, with a money return of $700,000. And the marvel of this shipment is the greater when it is brought to mind that this grand crop came from the ground that twenty years ago was reckoned to be the poorest land in the South, practically unsalable at any price. This was one of the sandy, stump-filled tracts from which the pine timber had been cut—too poor to grow cotton, corn or cane, and offered for years at the nominal rate of $1 per acre—without attracting any purchasers.

But with the keener study of the soil and some expert experimenting with fertilizers, the peculiar value of these cleared pine lands for small fruit growing was demonstrated. Peaches thrive, too, luxuriantly in the thin, red clay soil of the uplands, while strawberries, which can be grown in any soil of the region, ripen earliest in the sandy tracts. Hence these berries are frequently ready for market during the month of March, and the fruit continues to blossom and ripen for two full months and even longer. With the unflagging industry and care of the Italian berry growers, there will be an extraordinary expansion of small fruit-raising in the South during the next decade if proper measures are taken to secure and maintain contentedly the settlement of Italians on tracts available for this purpose.

This has been conclusively demonstrated by the advance of Independence and like plantations, for no particular advantages were offered for the assistance of the Italian settlers. On the contrary, Inspector Rossi reports that

An Italian Farmer's Home, Near Sunny Side, Arkansas

On Farm and Plantation

several tracts in Independence had been abandoned by the American farmers because they were too marshy and subject to floods. The keen-judging Italians bought these tracts at low prices and made them highly productive by drainage ditches, finally cutting a discharging canal three miles in length which is annually cleaned out. Almost all the Italian settlers are Sicilians from Palermo, and their good conduct and success is a signal attestation of the character and adaptive faculty which so many Southern Italians are showing in this country in the face of existing prejudice. "Every one of these families," as Signor Rossi records, "after paying all expenses, saved every year a few hundred dollars, which they deposited in the local American banks, sending a part of it to Italy. The material well-being of all could not possibly be greater."

In other highly important branches of agricultural industry in this country Italian immigrants have already made very notable advances also, not only in the results as yet attained, but in assurance for the future. To the extension and perfection of grape and olive growing particularly, they have made contributions of unquestionable importance.

A noteworthy success in this line, as well as in truck farming, has been attained by the Italian colony at Vineland, N. J., and its subsequent extensions to the adjoining townships of Landisville and Plainfield where more than 6,000 Italians are now profitably and prosperously employed. This colony was founded in 1878 by a few Italian peasants under the leadership of one of their own countrymen, who deserves an enduring memorial. This was the Chevalier Secchi de Casale, a disciple of Mazzini and a comrade of Garibaldi in his gallant fight for the independence of Italy. In 1849, when the struggle for freedom had failed for the time being, Signor de Casale fled to New York with some companions and made his home for a time on Staten Island in the Village of Stapleton. He soon established the first Italian newspaper in New York, L'Eco d'Italia, reaching with unflagging good cheer the sparsely sprinkled refugees of his nation in the United States, Canada and Mexico. He was an ever helpful counsellor and guardian to the poorest immigrant appealing to him for guidance and help. He was the first, too, to interpose signally for the protection of the poor little Italian street musicians who had been brought over and exploited for years by unscrupulous padroni. By the aid of the Italian consular and diplomatic representatives in this country he secured in 1874 the passage of an act by the Italian Parliament to abate this evil, and his efforts were seconded also by corresponding legislation in this country. He was very fitly knighted by King Victor Emmanuel in recognition of his services, and no Italian since the days of Columbus and the Cabots has been more worthy of commemoration for the keen-sighted intelligence and devotion of his services to the Italian in America.

On Farm and Plantation

He was the first to recognize actively here the importance of diverting the stream of Italian immigration to rural districts at the very outset of the rising of its flow. If he had been able to secure any wide-ranging co-operation, it is practically certain that he would have succeeded in the solution of the so-called "Italian problem" in this country. He was fortunate, however, in obtaining a signal demonstration of this fact through the hearty sympathy of one large American landowner, Mr. Charles Landis of Landisville, N. J. This public-spirited American put considerable tracts of land in Vineland and the neighborhood at the disposal of Signor de Casale for the development of his colonization scheme. This apparently weak little colony reached self-support and success within three years from its start. The Italians of Vineland were able to produce and market wine from their own plantations in 1881, and some wine is still made in this colony, though the efforts of the colonists have since been largely diverted to the more profitable occupation of truck farming and especially to the cultivation of sweet potatoes, a crop that has proved particularly desirable. The workers on these plantations, as a body, are unquestionably contented and prospering, and their success is sufficient proof of what might have been achieved by many like colonies elsewhere, if a like intelligent co-operation had been extended to them by American landowners.

Alessandro Mastro-Valerio is another patriotic Italian

who has carried Italian colonization onward with signal success in this country along the lines first deeply marked by Chevalier de Casale. The agricultural colonies which he established in succession, in the years 1890 and 1893, at Daphne and Lamberth, Alabama, are of peculiar interest in their pointing to the successful development of the South by Italian colonization. The foundation of the colony at Daphne was laid by him in the heart of an invigorating pine forest by the settlement of twenty Italian families on land bought at from $1.50 to $5.00 per acre. The allotment for each family was from 25 to 50 acres. The growth of pines was cleared away by degrees, and the colonists used the lumber which they cut from their own trees to build their houses. Mr. Mastro-Valerio was then conducting experiments for the United States Department of Agriculture, and the "Alabama State Experiment Station," and was able to give to the colonists all needed instruction in the planting and care of the vineyards which he planned for them. From the outset he inspired their efforts unflaggingly and made it possible for them to overcome the inevitable difficulties and endure the trying privations of pioneer colonization. The vines and fruit trees, expertly laid out in a neatly ordered system of rows and stakes, have thrived remarkably, and their fruit is brought to an unusually early maturity so that the vintage is ended by the 10th of July, and uncrushed grapes can be shipped to the Northern market where they command a price as high as 15 cents a pound. The demand for this shipment has been such that some choice varieties of European vines producing grapes for the table have been grafted on native stock, and this hybrid product has proved very attractive and appetizing. The sale of these grapes is constantly extending, and wine of excellent quality has already been made in quantity for market, and both demand and product are surely extending.

While awaiting the maturing of the vineyards and fruit trees, the same intelligent director pushed forward from the start the production of vegetables marketable from the end of the first season for the livelihood of the colonists. The soil of Daphne is sandy, with a red or yellow subsoil, and has the advantage of being easily worked, a very important feature to colonists with little capital and simple tools of husbandry. It is not fertile, and would hardly warrant cultivation without the use of artificial fertilizers, but this was foreseen by the promoter of the colony and the needed fertilization was determined and provided. On the cleared lands wheat, corn, rice, tobacco, cotton, oats, peanuts, Irish and sweet potatoes and other vegetables were successfully grown, and the whole district is now luxuriantly productive, sometimes yielding two crops in a year.

These colonist families are, without exception, contented and thrifty. The climate is remarkably healthy. The ozone and aroma of the pines are delightful and invigorating. Winter snows rarely fall on this favored land, and the summer heat is tempered by the constant breeze from the Gulf of Mexico. Occasional frost is the only plague which colonists have to fear, and its blight is expertly avoided in the coldest nights of March by ranges of open-air fires consuming little hillocks of damp leaves and grass sprinkled with petroleum. The colony now possesses a school and church of its own, and its noteworthy thrift and success have been repeatedly remarked by interested visitors and the representative newspapers of Daphne and Mobile.

The colony of Lamberth was established to meet the selection of Italians who wished to settle along the line of the Mobile and Ohio Railway in Mobile County. This colony has now more than a dozen families of very prosperous people, successfully engaged in viticulture and in truck farming. They have built a church and school and secured a railway station at their plantation. Their development has been so closely correspondent to that of the larger colony of Daphne under the same direction that it is unnecessary to particularize its methods of progress.

The success of these typical colonies unquestionably shows what might be effected without much difficulty through this plan of distribution if it could be prosecuted on a great scale with efficient co-operation, but this, unfortunately, cannot be assured, and it is, therefore, of more immediate practical interest to note what has been effected thus far by an almost unaided movement of distribution. This appears in the thriving vineyards of the wine belt of New York, Pennsylvania and Ohio where Italian labor is now largely employed and where the advance of Italian ownership is steadily if not rapidly progressing. Here the object-lesson doesn't require the provision of special means for its extension, the Italian beginning as a hired laborer under appreciative employers and gradually advancing to the self-supported assertion of independence.

The advance of the Italians in the agricultural settlements of California suffices to show the prospect that is open to such a laborer under favoring conditions. In view of his unhappy experience at home it will be generally easier also to induce the Italian cafoni who land here as immigrants to go upon the land with the certainty of fixed wages at the outset, a weekly return in cash which they can see and handle, than to hold up to them the less tangible prospects of profit sharing on a co-operative basis or the promise of land with indefinite burdens to be assumed before its ownership is secured to them. This was notably demonstrated in the planting of the now famous colony of Asti in Sonoma County, California.

Here the organizers were chiefly enterprising Italians of San Francisco who were able to command sufficient means for the establishment of a promising colony. They raised a capital of $10,000, and then appointed a committee of three directors to select the most desirable location for a vineyard. The prime motive of this undertaking was distinctly philanthropic, as its originators were not looking for personal profit but were moved by the desire of providing a good livelihood and prospects for the poor Italians in San Francisco who were finding it difficult to obtain steady employment. After an exhaustive examination the committee selected a tract of fifteen hundred acres of rolling hill land not subject to drought and excellently well adapted for viticulture, and accessible by railway at a distance of a little more than a hundred miles from San Francisco. They named the chosen spot Asti in memory of the ancient Asti in Piedmont, whose product of wine has been for centuries a source of pride to its citizens.

The first cost of the land to the Association was $25,000, and to secure clear title its members were obliged to pay down at once the subscription in their treasury and raise an additional $15,000 at the rate of $1,000 a month for fifteen months thereafter. This they did, and then further capital was needed and provided to clear the sheep range, which they had bought, of immense oak trees and roots, and prepare the land for setting out grape cuttings.

In the By-Laws of the Association preference for permanent employment was given to Italian-Swiss persons who were either citizens of the United States or had declared their intention to become citizens. This article was intended to secure permanence of settlement and benefit to the laborers. Provision was made for the payment of wages ranging from $30 to $40 per month in addition to sleeping quarters, good board and as much wine as they cared to drink. This proposal was on its face attractive enough for any Italian laborer in the city, and there would not have been the least difficulty in filling up the possible quota of laborers to the limit had it not been coupled with a proviso requiring each laborer to subscribe to at least five shares of stock in the Association, in payment for which a deduction of $5.00 per month would be withheld from his wages. He would thus be interested in the profits of the enterprise and on a relatively equal footing of dignity and control with the leading proprietors or share owners. Moreover, this subscription, if he so desired, when the land became fruitful, would entitle him to receive a number of acres to own and develop independently. To any American laborer this requirement would, of course, seem at the worst an inconsiderable drawback, even if its prospective benefits were not keenly appreciated. But the poor Italians, one and all, failed to understand it or were suspicious of a possible cheat or perilous liability in it. Hence it is a matter of record that not a single laborer could be induced to go to work under the compulsion to take even a share of stock in the Association. Thus the organizers were obliged to dispose of this allotment of stock to other

137

subscribers and to pay their laborers wholly in cash, thereby defeating at the outset the cherished aim of the Association for the improvement of the condition of the laborer.

It must be conceded, however, that for a number of years the actual progress and returns of the undertaking seemed to justify the scepticism of the laborers. The preparation of the soil was steadily continued and choice grape cuttings were imported from Italy, France, Hungary and the valley of the Rhine through an interested co-operator, Dr. G. Olino of Asti, Italy. These cuttings were received in good condition and set out on the land of the company under the direction of an expert. When the vines came into prolific bearing, however, the Association was obliged to face a grave disappointment. At the time of the organization of the Association the market price of grapes from California was $30.00 per ton, a rate that was a certain guarantee of very large profits. But when the grapes from the Association were ready for marketing, the price had fallen to $8.00 per ton, a return which didn't even meet the cost of growing the product.

Hence it was necessary to suspend operations, or else to extend the plan of production by undertaking the manufacture of wine on the ground. Meanwhile the required monthly payment had been continued for five years, and every shareholder had been obliged to pay $60.00 a share for his stock, raising the capital invested thus far to $150,000. The call for the building of a stone winery of adequate capacity then entailed a further assessment of $10.00 per share, with which the needed establishment was built and wine produced for market. Even then, at the outset, the undertaking seemed doomed to failure. The best price that could be obtained for the wine from dealers in California was only 7 cents per gallon, a return below the cost of production, and if the energetic directors of the Association had not persisted in seeking a better price by shipping their product in quantity to dealers in New Orleans, Chicago, New York and other principal markets, their venture would have collapsed inevitably. Fortunately their faith and persistence were justified by the judgment of the leading dealers of the country and the appreciation of consumers. They succeeded in selling their product at prices ranging from 30 to 50 cents per gallon, according to quality, and a steady and profitable demand was thenceforth assured.

Moreover, the able controllers of the Association had the exceptional patience and judgment requisite to conduct their business with the view primarily of perfecting their product to the farthest attainable point without sacrificing its quality for the sake of immediate cash returns. They continued to sell, year by year, only enough of their product to pay running expenses and the enlargements essential for the development of the business. The balance of the wines was stored in their vaults and expertly matured. It was only after sixteen years of this patient perfecting that the Association began for the first time to pay a dividend to its stockholders, but subsequent returns have richly rewarded their patience. A continuous succession of large dividends has been paid, and these returns and the known value of the property have raised the value of the shares to three times their original cost to the investors. The Association has now the largest dry wine vineyard in California and a great winery completely fitted with the best modern equipment. The best wine-producing grapes are perfected, including the leading Italian varieties, such as the Freisa, Grignolino, Barolo, Barbera and Chianti. In this winery for two months in the year 300 tons of grapes are pressed daily. Immense glass vats, each holding 120,000 litres, receive the product, and there are never less than from 6,000 to 7,000 barrels in the warehouses.

Here the principal Italian wines and the red and white wines of France and Germany are now produced, besides sweet wines in great variety and extra dry champagnes for the American market. It is also producing what is reported to be a very superior quality of brandy and cognac, including the favorite Grappa of the Italian people, which is said to be identical in flavor and taste with that made in the mother country. For the past ten years the establishment has been employing more than two hundred laborers daily, and at the time of the harvest, which lasts two months, many hundreds more are engaged. The colony has long been a most thriving settlement with many families and happy homes, a well-built and well-conducted school and complete post office, telephone and telegraphic communications. Its carefully matured product of wines is now shipped daily to all parts of Central and South America, China and Japan, and in very considerable quantity to England, Germany, Switzerland and Belgium, and even to the ports of Southern France where it bears favorable comparison, it is said, with the standard French wines.

There is an extraordinary resemblance of the hills of Asti to those of the historic Asti in Italy, from which it takes its name. Its beauty strikes the eye of every visitor, and the artistic villas on its hillsides, chiefly owned by members of the Italian-Swiss Association, are among the most charming residences in California. Three of the leading members are particularly distinguished in the report of Signor Rossi. Cav. A. Sbarboro, native of Genoa, came here as a boy and laid the foundation of his fortune in the promotion of the colony by establishing co-operative banks. Through this undertaking, by the contribution for investment of a small sum monthly, resident families obtained loans to build houses and for other enterprises. Cav. Pietro C. Rossi, a distinguished pharmacist and graduate of the University of Turin, was first engaged in business in America in the drug line. Dr. De Vecchi entered the Italian-Swiss Colony at its most critical period and began the practice of his profession in San Francisco as a surgeon in 1880. His competence was so pronounced that from the start his income was very large, and in the third year of his practice it reached the amount of $34,000.

A large extension of the establishments of the same Association has been made at Madera in Southern California, one hundred and eighty-four miles from San Francisco. Here 2,000 acres of rich soil are now producing about five million pounds of grapes annually, and there is another completely equipped winery where port, sherry Muscat and Angelica and other sweet wines of high quality are made as well as a considerable amount of brandy. The Madera establishment has been connected by a special railway branch with the town, four miles distant, and is reported to possess machinery for grape-crushing and brandy-making unexcelled by any in the world.

At harvest time two hundred persons are employed, according to Signor Rossi's latest report. In the other months of the year from forty to fifty Italians do the requisite work, receiving on an average wages of from $1.25 to $1.50 per day in addition to lodging and food. The meals are said to be very abundant, the workmen getting three a day in which meat, bread, eggs, vegetables and wine are served. There is no limitation to the amount of wine allowed, but any workman who gets drunk is discharged, though this happens very rarely. In the vast cellars of this establishment there are casks of a capacity of 150,000 litres. Outside its own grapes, the society makes wine from many others bought from its neighbors. At the time of its foundation the Association owning this great establishment was called The Italian-Swiss because among its stockholders there were some Swiss of the Canton Ticino. To-day it is entirely Italian. Its director, a native of Piedmont, is reported to be undoubtedly a most competent specialist not only in the cultivation of the vines but also in the production and maturing of wine.

The remarkable success of this Association is of far-reaching influence and value in its demonstration of the feasibility of producing wines of high quality in this country on a great scale, and of extending a great field of employment for which the Italian immigrant labor is particularly adapted. Other undertakings of the same kind with which Italians have been more or less fully identified have achieved an almost equally gratifying measure of success. Perhaps more than any other State in the Union, California resembles Italy in climate and soil, and it is natural that the vineyard developments there should first have been pushed on a great scale by Italian labor. There is not a Californian valley to-day where there is not a dozen or more Italian farms, fruit orchards or vineyards, and large numbers of Italians are now employed and preferred by American farmers. The truck farmers around the Californian cities are mostly Italian, and their success in every variety of farming employment in that State is now indisputable.

The reckoning of the number of Italians who, with scarcely an exception, are thriving in the State, which was prepared by the Italian Chamber of Commerce of San Francisco in 1897, is greatly in excess of the latest national census returns, as all persons of Italian descent born in this country are included. This report states that 45,625 Italians were then living in the 56 counties of California, and that almost all of them were engaged in agriculture, a convincing proof that the drift to the towns and to other pursuits was not uncontrollable. They were credited with owning 2,726 farms, orchards, vineyards, ranches, etc., and there were in addition 837 Italian business concerns with a capital of $17,908,300.

The particular adaptability of the Italians to the rising requirements for labor in the cotton, rice and sugar-cane districts is becoming more generally recognized. Already there is a marked preference for Italian in place of negro labor on the sugar-cane plantations of Louisiana and Mississippi. The system of employment is, in the main, excellent. The plantations are often divided into separate tracts, each assigned to a separate family for cultivation. A fixed rent is placed on the land and the necessary animals and tools for cultivation are provided by the proprietor, who furnishes also, when required, an advance of provisions for the season or the guarantee of credit to

NEW GROUND COTTON

Cultivated by Italian Settlers Near Sunny Side, Arkansas

the necessary extent at the nearest supply store. At the end of the season he buys the sugar cane at market rates and pays over the price to the laborers, having first deducted his rent and advances. This is an incitement to the best feasible production and seems preferable on the whole to the metayer or half-share system, as the laborer is thus assured of obtaining all that he earns if the accounting is fair, and this is well guaranteed by the competition for labor and the desire to hold a good cane-grower continuously.

Thousands of Italians are now going yearly from our Central and Northern States, as well as directly from Italy, to these plantations in the season for cane-cutting to assist the cultivators in the harvest and returning in spring to other employment in the Northern States. Most of these Italians come from Sicily or Southern Italy, and nothing seriously objectionable is noted in their character and work. In fact, they have proved themselves to be exceptionally reliable in their engagements and industry, and their services have practically become indispensable.

In a previous chapter it has been shown that the growth of cotton in Southern Italy has been largely advancing of late years. A noteworthy illustration of the adaptability of the Southern Italian to this branch of agriculture and of the natural method by which he may be diverted to it is given in the founding of the colony of Bryan in Brazos County, Texas, before described. About twenty-five years ago some Sicilians were hired to work on the main branch of the Houston and Texas Railroad. When the work to which they had been called had been finished they were induced to buy some land on the Brazos River, which was sold cheaply because it was subject to inundation, though otherwise desirable. Their undertaking was profitable almost from the outset, and in subsequent years the addition of relatives and friends has swelled the numbers in the colony to over two thousand, cultivating both cotton and corn with signal success.

In the neighborhood of Greenville, Mississippi, on the line of the Illinois Central Railroad, there is another group of cotton plantations and truck farms all owned and successfully operated by Italians, now numbering from seventy to eighty families. In the late report of Inspector Rossi all these settlers were credited with "noteworthy gains," and all were said to enjoy good health, "except for the inconvenience of some malarial fever to which they were subject in the months of August and September." This local and temporary fever is the only noted drawback to settlement in the Yazoo Delta, "that most spacious valley" of two millions of acres lying between the Mississippi and Yazoo rivers which, as the official inspector reports, "is truly of extraordinary fertility."

It is indeed probable that this delta contains the richest undeveloped agricultural territory in the world, and its certain yield when cultivated is becoming so widely appreciated that land now purchasable at from ten to fifteen dollars per acre will before long be quadrupled in market value at least. The "inconvenience of fever" can be successfully overcome by simple precautions which experienced settlers now take and which should be insistently urged upon all newcomers, especially the Italians, who are apt to be imprudently neglectful of the first principles of healthful living. This was particularly observed by an intelligent Italian settler on the great plantation originally founded by Austin Corbin and Prince Ruspoli, then Mayor of Rome, at Sunnyside on the banks of the Mississippi, some twenty miles below Greenville. "Our countrymen settled here," he stated to the inspector, "do not take hygienic precautions of any kind. They will not boil their drinking water, and in the morning they walk barefooted in the dew." It does not seem credible that this recklessness should be stubbornly persisted in if the Italian settlers and newcomers are properly warned and impressed, and it would be a grievous error if the grand opening in this virgin field should be stupidly passed by through any ill-grounded prejudice or apprehension.

The attraction of this region for Italian colonization and its assurance of success are demonstrated in particular, upon the Sessions plantation in Coahoma County, Mississippi, about eighty miles from Memphis. Here a dozen Italian families have been residing for years who are cultivating cotton fields on "half shares." The heads of these families reported to Inspector Rossi that they were well contented, but that, in general, after some years of experience with the "half-share" system, the Italian preferred to acquire lands to cultivate for his own account. This is natural and usually feasible. The lack of school facilities and the high cost of medical aid owing to the distance of the plantation from the nearest town were the only noted complaints here, both of which may readily be remedied through the willingness of the owner of the plantation to take immediately two hundred Italian families on half shares. He greatly preferred Italian labor from his experience to that of the negro.

The largest settlement of Italians in this region on the notable Austin Corbin plantation at Sunnyside is of peculiar interest in the opportunity that it affords for the direct comparison of the efficiency of Italian and negro labor working under absolutely equal conditions on the same plantation. This plantation is now operated under lease from the Corbin estate by Mr. C. B. Crittenden and Mr. Leroy Percy of Greenville, Mississippi. There are about 11,000 acres in the plantation, nearly half of which are in cultivation for the production of cotton. The cotton fields are worked by about ninety Italian families, and substantially the same number of negro families. The greater part of the Italian families are natives of the Marches in Italy, and form a colony numbering about five hundred in all. A young priest from the Marches came to the colony last year as curate in response to a request from the Bishop of Arkansas to the Bishop of Sinigaglia.

It was reported to Signor Rossi by Mr. Crittenden that, with a single exception, every family on the plantation was working successfully.

The plan of operation is substantially as follows: At the beginning of the season an account is opened with each tenant at the plantation store. He is first charged up with $7.00 per acre rental for as many acres as the family judge they can cultivate. For each mule supplied to the tenant a rental of $25 per year is charged, and there is a small additional rental for the use of machinery. If a bill for medical attendance has been incurred during the year that is also charged in the account, and all supplies necessary for the house and barn are included.

At the end of the season cotton is purchased by the planters, and if the cotton crop amounts to more than is shown on the ledger account for advances, the tenant gets a check on the bank for the difference. The following figures are taken direct from the ledger showing the net return to eight separate Italian families for the year 1903:

One family that worked 20 acres in cotton received a check for $517 00
Another family that worked 19 acres in cotton received a
check for... 714 59
Another family that worked 33 acres in cotton received a
check for... 1,211 36
Another family that worked 30 acres in cotton received a
check for... 579 60

Another family that worked 14 acres in cotton received a
check for.. $512 98
Another family that worked 17 acres in cotton received a
check for.. 738 15
Another family that worked 30 acres in cotton received a
check for.. 1,142 05
Another family that worked 35 acres in cotton received a
check for.. 1,358 63

One of the managers of this plantation, Mr. Leroy
Percy, reports in the Southern Farm Magazine (May,
1904) that some of the Italians have been upon the plantation for years, and that the number is increasing yearly.
The managers "advanced to the Italians upon the property during the past year $4,000 or $5,000, with which
they brought over their friends and relatives from Italy, and
all of which was paid back by them out of the past crop.

"As growers of cotton they are in every respect superior
to the negro. They are industrious and thrifty, though
the present generation will not develop the land-owning
instinct; they all dream of returning to Sunny Italy. The
property is worked about one-half by negroes and one-
half by Italians. There doesn't seem to be any race antagonism between them and no race mixture.

"The Italians make a profit of $5.00 out of a crop where
the negro makes $1.00, and yet the negro seems to be
perfectly satisfied with his returns. No spirit of emula-
tion is excited by the superior work or prosperity of his
Italian neighbor. We had one of them recently return
to Italy with more than $8,000 in cash, never having

worked more than thirty acres of land, leaving behind him a family to work the land and with sufficient money to provide themselves for another year."

The increase of the negroes in the South at large, Mr. Percy states, "is entirely insufficient to meet the increased demands upon them created by the double tracking and improving of roads, the increase in oil mills, saw mills, and similar enterprises, and the increasing demand for labor to clear up the land, greatly stimulated as this is by the present prices of cotton."

The problem that must be solved in the Mississippi delta, in his view, "is the obtaining of some other labor to do what the present race of negroes is unable to do. The only practical solution to the problem that offers itself to my mind is the encouragement of the immigration of Italians." In conclusion, he affirms again with emphasis: "If the immigration of these people is encouraged, they will gradually take the place of the negro without there being any such violent change as to paralyze for a generation the prosperity of the country."

Probably the most acute investigation and forecast of Italian labor in the cotton fields of the South has been made by Alfred Holt Stone, who reports his conclusions in a recent number of the South Atlantic Quarterly under the caption, "The Italian Cotton Grower; The Negro's Problem." It might fairly be assumed that in no section of the South is negro labor more firmly en-

trenched than in the riparian lands of the Mississippi and
its tributaries, in Arkansas, Mississippi and Louisiana.
Here the negroes outnumber the whites in the proportion
of from three or four to one to more than fifteen to one.
"Every condition of climate, soil and economic condition
tended," as Mr. Stone observes, "to render absolute the
hold of the negro agriculturist." Yet Italian cotton
growers have already entered this field of negro monopoly,
and their assured advance has already demonstrated the
marked superiority of Italian labor. In the course of a
year or two Mr. Stone reports that they become more intelligent cultivators than the negroes. They work more
carefully and constantly. Tenants, like the negroes, they
keep the fields and premises in so much better condition
that a passerby may see at a glance whether the occupant
is an Italian or a negro. The fields of the latter are half
cultivated, his fences broken down, his garden choked with
weeds. From his personal experience in the cultivation
of plantations in which he is interested as an owner, he
says that it seems hopeless to try to induce negro tenants
to keep the premises in good order and repair.

Of Italian labor, on the other hand, on these and the
like plantations, Mr. Stone bears expert witness. "From
the garden spot which the negro allows to grow up in
weeds, the Italian will supply his family from early spring
until late fall, and also market enough largely to carry
him through the winter. I have seen the ceilings of their

houses literally covered with strings of dried butter beans, peppers, okra and other garden products, while the walls would be hung with corn, sun-cured in the roasting ear stage. In the rear of a well-kept house would be erected a woodshed, and in it could be seen enough firewood, sawed and ready for use, to run the family through the winter months. These people didn't wait till half frozen feet compelled attention to the question of fuel and then tear down a fence to supply their wants. Nor would they be found drifting about near the close of each season in an aimless effort to satisfy an unreasoned desire to 'move,' to make the next crop somewhere else."

In his own relatively thickly settled country, where the land suitable for cultivation has been so rigidly monopolized and so grudgingly yielded to small proprietors, the Italian has been forced by the experience of centuries to make the most of every inch of his ground, and this inured habit persists in his practice in this country. What is too small for the plow he cultivates with a hoe. He sows down to the water's edge. Mr. Stone has seen Italians "make more cotton per acre than the negro on the adjoining cut, gather it from two to four weeks earlier, and then put in the extra time in earning money by picking in the negro's field."

The adaptability of the Italian to work in the rice fields is no less certain than his desirability to meet the demands of the sugar cane and cotton planters. Many Italians are now engaged in the culture of rice, in the rice fields of South-eastern Texas, and the extension of encouragement in feasible ways is all that is required to attract Italians very largely to the opportunities open in this and other Southern states.

Of course any large displacing of negro labor or considerable influx of Italian immigrants into the "black belts" of the South will be necessarily the outcome of years of immigration, if effected at all. The industrious negro need have no fear that his labor will be supplanted by any possible influx in a way to threaten his employment or progress. It will be a positive advantage, on the other hand, to the hard working negro as well as to the white planters of the South, if the lazy and shiftless negro should be forced by such competition to steadier work and to habits of economy and rational prudence. As a matter of fact, the uncultivated area lying open for entry and profitable production is still so vast, and the demand for the products of the South so far outruns the supply that there is no likelihood of any pressure of competition from the influx of Italian or other immigrant labor, for years to come, sufficient to effect any material regeneration in the industry or life of the negro. The most that can sanely be hoped for is the relief of the South from entire dependence on the shaky and insufficient prop of negro labor and the mingling of sufficient white settlers to dissipate somewhat the hanging cloud of negro dominance and assure a progress otherwise unattainable. ELIOT LORD.

CHAPTER VIII

In view of the proven adaptability of the Italian here, even under adverse conditions, for varied occupations and specially for intensive farming, there can be no questioning of a rising demand for his labor except upon the baldly jealous assumption that the labor supply of the country exceeds its demand and that any importation of labor will necessarily displace American laborers now employed and narrow the opportunities of those seeking employment. This assumption is often a bitter contention of labor unions, but it cannot bear submission to the opposition of facts.

Let it simply be recalled that little Belgium in proportion to its area is supporting now a population to the square mile twenty-five times as large as the United States, without groaning audibly under the pressure. The Lone Star State alone, in this country, has double the area of Italy, yet it is maintaining a population to-day only one-tenth as great. To extend the comparison broadly, it may be noted that the average density of population in the United States is only one-fourteenth of the density of population per square mile in Italy. Yet Italy is now complaining of the drain of its working force by immigration, though in natural resources and means of development it cannot bear comparison for a moment to our own prolific and wealthy country. Temporarily strained and distressful conditions and the existence of a few congested centres offer no substantial grounds for any contention of over-population or an overplus of labor in our country at large. The sanely economic remedy for these local and occasional evils assuredly lies in the perfecting of a better distribution—not in the choking off of the productive flow of labor for our national development.

If the existence of open ground for this distribution and profitable employment is still questionable in the mind of anybody, let him examine as a single object lesson the proportion of unimproved to improved land in the South. This was lately emphasized with striking force in the speech of Hon. Wyatt Aiken of South Carolina in the House of Representatives, April 22, 1904, in support of his bill (H. R. 14833) authorizing the Commissioner-General of Immigration to establish an information bureau on Ellis Island " for the better enlightenment of immigrants and for their better distribution throughout this land." " The land area of the South," he observed, " is 585,310,000 acres." " In 1900 the total farm acreage was 387,690,426 acres. The total improved acreage was only 145,185,599. This leaves about 242,000,000 acres of farm lands to be put into profitable cultivation."

Rising Demand for Italian Immigrant Labor

" The unimproved farm lands of the South give a greater area for settlement and cultivation than the total area of Texas, Louisiana, and Arkansas combined. Over 110,000,000 acres of this land lies east of the Mississippi River, and there is comparatively a small amount of it which is not available for crops of some kind. For diversity, quantity, and quality of productions the Southern States are unsurpassed. Mr. Wilson, Secretary of Agriculture, after touring the South, said: ' No section of the world offers such inducements for diversified farming; ' and he predicted a future for that section such as has not been witnessed before in this country."

" That our people grow cotton almost exclusively is due to the fact that at prevailing prices it is the most profitable and merchantable crop that is planted. Where the farmer turns his attention to diversified crops, the results compare favorably with the best efforts of farmers without this region."

As to the character of immigration desired or the nationalities particularly adaptable to the needs of the South, Mr. Aiken further remarked, " until lately, considerable prejudice existed against the Italian, but with most favorable testimony in his behalf from Georgia, Louisiana, and a number of other Southern States, our people look with a great deal more favor on these hardy, industrious agriculturists."

If it be conceded that undeniable statistics demonstrate

157

the relative paucity of population to the square mile in this country and the vast extent of lands, yet unimproved and open for development, it may still be urged that the influx of immigration in recent years exceeds our capacity to handle and distribute. This is indeed a common contention of alarmists, who seemingly prefer sensation to facts. A single punch, such as the one lately given by the "Philadelphia Record," is sufficient to smash the hollow shell of contention. The " Record " observes editorially (June 21, 1904), " whether from mere carelessness or from design, the most exaggerated and false assertions are made concerning the great flood of immigration, as if the like had never before been witnessed in the history of this country. During the years 1880, 1881, 1882 and 1883 the total immigration to the United States amounted to 2,519,-202 persons. During the last four years the total number of immigrant arrivals was 2,442,279.

" Twenty years ago the population of the United States amounted to 50,000,000, and now it is about 80,000,000, exclusive of the Philippines. So the immigration relatively is not nearly so great now as it was in the former period. But this is not all. Twenty years ago comparatively few immigrants returned to their native land because of the time and cost of the voyage. Now they are swiftly carried back in great numbers by every European steamer, some to stay, and some for a longer or shorter visit. When the balance comes to be struck, the annual increase of immigrant population is very small compared with that of former years."

A noted fluctuation ranging only from one year to another is not usually of any material account as a measure of the flow of immigration, but, in view of any possible swell of apprehension, without examination of facts, it may be well to note the marked falling off of immigration to this country and the increase in emigration in comparative records of the first six months of 1904 and 1903. The official bulletin of the North Atlantic Steamship Conference shows that between January 1st and June 17 of the latter year, 118,484 fewer passengers came here in the steerage of the various lines than for the same period last year. There was further a noted increase of 31,538 steerage passengers sailing from the port of New York during the same period. Thus exact examination demonstrates that there was really more cause to apprehend a comparative dearth of immigration than an overflow.

In face of these facts there remains only the rickety prop of contention, that, whether the influx be great or small, it is no longer wanted in this country. This has been pushed even to the utter disregard of the character of the influx by influential voices of opinion. One of the most able and dignified of these may be cited as typical. The well known president of the United Mine Workers, Mr. John Mitchell, has declared in a recent address, " No matter how decent and self-respecting and hard working

The Italian in America

the aliens who are flooding this country may be, they are invading the land of Americans, and whether they know it or not, are helping to take the bread out of their mouths. America for Americans should be the motto of every citizen, whether he be a working man or a capitalist. There are already too many aliens in this country. There is not enough work for the many millions of unskilled laborers, and there is no need for the added millions who are pressing into our cities and towns to compete with the skilled American in his various trades and occupations. While the majority of the immigrants are not skilled workmen, they rapidly become so, and their competition is not of a stimulating order." *

This strain of exclusion sounds cracked in the mouth of the son of an immigrant. The policy that he advocates would have shut out his father and precluded his own birth in this country and the possibility of his objection to the sharing of its opportunities. Moreover, careful examination shows that his assumptions are incorrect. The entry of unskilled labor does not diminish the opportunities open to American skilled labor. On the contrary, it greatly expands them.

The most progressive manufacturing and commercial cities in the East are those which have received the greatest influx of immigration comparatively in recent years. Instead of taking away the jobs and reducing the number

* New York Times, January 17, 1904.

Market Day at Independence, Louisiana. A Thriving Italian Settlement

Rising Demand for Italian Immigrant Labor

of American native workmen employed, there is not a single instance in which the influx has not operated to enlarge the demand for American skilled labor and increase the number of skilled American workmen actually employed. The reliable provision of a supply of unskilled labor has directly led to the establishment of handlers and converters of raw materials, thus affording a securer basis for the supply and development of manufactures in which skilled labor constitutes the chief percentage of cost. Wide ranging investigation demonstrates that the mass of immigrant labor in recent years has not yet been raised to competition with skilled operatives and that their employment is affording an essential basis for the expansion and maintenance of the manufactures of advanced labor products.

The application of " raw " immigrant labor, too, in railway grading and extensions and in public works of all kinds necessarily leads to the expansion of industry, employing laborers in numbers far exceeding the total of pioneer labor employed. The planning and execution of railway development, for example, depend materially on the estimated cost of materials and labor and the certainty of the supply of both. The influx of immigrant labor affords the only substantial assurance of the maintenance of this supply, and the stoppage of this influx would assuredly curtail railway building, road improvements and State and municipal public works throughout this country.

The Italian in America

It is not difficult to account for the fact that immigrants of late years have been coming chiefly from the Southern rather than from the Northern countries of Europe. The more complete the educational system of any country, the greater the number of skilled laborers that is produced and the fewer the number of unskilled laborers. In the United States, at present, the number of unskilled laborers is constantly and rapidly decreasing and the like may be said of Germany, France, Great Britain and the Scandinavian countries. Hence, the common laborers required for the unskilled labor supply of this country are drawn naturally from those countries whose systems of education are less complete or where racial discrimination exists, and the influx necessarily rises in proportion to the withdrawal of Americans and the northern races of Europe from the lower grades of labor. The ambitious and educated American will not do the low grade work. The English, Germans and Scandinavians, and of late years even the Irish, have risen or are rising above it. It is therefore inevitable that we must look for an adequate supply of unskilled labor to the countries whose inhabitants are willing to fill the demand with the prospect before them of steady employment and certain advancement for themselves and their children.

In practical confirmation of this position, it is to be noted, too, that there has never been a period in the history of this country when the urgency of the call for labor for the development of our resources has been so out-spoken and pronounced. There has been heretofore surprisingly little organized or artificial encouragement of immigration to this country. " The truth is," as Dr. Edward Everett Hale observed pointedly, ten years ago, in a contribution to " The Social Economist," " that the wave of immigration has come without our asking for it; it has enriched us without our care, and, speaking for organizations, whether of churches, or of States, we have let it alone with a sublime indifference which would hardly be conceived possible, if it were not everywhere apparent."

In face of this apparent listlessness, the Dominion of Canada has, of late years, been putting up an object lesson in the organization and determination of its efforts for the attraction of immigration. The Canadian Commissioner of Immigration reported in 1903 that up to October 1st, 122,141 immigrants settled in Manitoba alone in the preceding nine months, more than double the number of incomers during the same period in 1902. It was anticipated in that year that the influx into the Canadian West and Northwest would be doubled, at least, in 1903, and this expectation was fully realized.

Yet, not content with this influx, the Dominion Government has been more energetic than ever in its efforts to attract immigration. It widely advertised in 1903 that 257,410,000 acres available for settlement still remained at the disposal of the Government and other land agencies in Assiniboia, Alberta, Saskatchewan and Athabasca. To this should be added the 74,000,000 acres available in Manitoba, and it will be seen at a glance how vast an area north of our boundary line is now readily open and even clamoring for settlement. Lists of Dominion agents and sub-agents in Western Canada have been scattered broadcast, and in most of our own Northern States there are specially engaged agents who are expected to circulate the Government publications and other advertisements for settlers and to promote in every feasible way by their personal effort an influx of immigration across the line.

On the 1st of May in 1904 the reported number of these regularly commissioned agents actively employed in the United States was seventy-five. In addition to this force there were several hundred sub-agents, receiving a per capita fee on the emigrants booked for Canada of $3 for each adult male, $2 for each adult female and $1 for every child under 12 years of age. There were further employed by the Government about 350 agents in Great Britain, receiving $1.68 for every adult and 84 cents for every child booked for Canada. The total expenditure by the Canadian Government in 1903 to promote immigration was stated to be $642,913. This disbursement may be contrasted instructively with the outlay by our own government of not a single dollar for this purpose, and the fact that even the expenses for the exclusion of undesirable immigrants are wholly defrayed by the entering immigrants, without imposing the charge of a cent upon the government or people of this country.

Under the pointed head lines: " Canada Out-Hustles Uncle Sam."—" Draws More Immigrants from United Kingdom this Year than U. S.," the watchful " New York Sun " noted the first fruits of this outlay in a despatch from its London correspondent, dated May 8, 1904.

" For the first time on record the emigration from the United Kingdom to Canada bids fair this year to exceed that to the United States. Last year, says W. T. R. Preston, the Canadian Commissioner of Emigration here, 57,000 persons emigrated from this country to Canada, while to the United States there went 67,000. Thus far this year the number of emigrants who have left these shores for Canada is in excess of that for a like period last year, and in the summer it is expected the ratio of increase will be much greater.

" While Uncle Sam does nothing to attract emigrants from this country Canada is hustling to get them, and meeting with such success that other colonies of the empire have been moved to envy and are bestirring themselves to follow her example and copy her methods."

" ' England,' said Mr. Preston to the writer, ' is the only European country possessing colonies that devotes neither efforts nor money to encouraging emigration to them. What England won't do for us Canada is doing for herself. It costs something, of course, but it is the best paying investment that Canada ever made. Last year we expended $300,000 in working up emigration from this country to Canada. We distributed 1,500,000 pamphlets, kept a lot of agents on the jump and spent a pile of money in advertising. But not a dollar went in the shape of passage money. We are not sending any deadheads to Canada.' "

*   *   *   *   *   *   *   *

" Situated in Charing Cross, in one of the broadest thoroughfares of London, the Canadian Government emigration offices are admirably located to attract attention, and the most is made of the opportunities. Besides the big London offices, Canadian agencies are established in Liverpool, Birmingham, Glasgow, Dublin, Belfast and Cardiff. Advertising is done on a large scale and effectively, the alluring promise of ' Free Farms for Willing Workers ' often extending across the whole front page of a newspaper."

The progress of this propaganda and a somewhat pretentious formation at St. Paul, Minnesota, of the Western Canada Immigration Association, for the purpose of stimulating American immigration to the prairie wheat fields of Canada, have seriously alarmed our own wheat producing States at the drain of settlers. Minnesota has already taken steps to rebut this drain and stimulate immigration by the holding of a representative convention which adopted resolutions constituting itself a State Immigration

Rising Demand for Italian Immigrant Labor

Society and appealing for the establishment of a State Bureau of Immigration. In the able discussions of the situation, a strong presentation was made of the present imperative needs of Minnesota for the further development of her farm lands and the extension of the diversification of her agricultural industries. It was pointed out that in fruit production in the last decade, Minnesota made the greatest progress of any State in the Union, according to the last census, and that no other State afforded better opportunities for the possible engagement of capital and labor in this line of development. The amount of potatoes and other vegetables grown in the State was also increasing annually and the most confident anticipation was expressed of the great feasible increase of this product.

The call for the development of Minnesota's dairy products was even more emphatically marked.

" A great empire in Northern Minnesota," said W. W. P. McConnell, State Dairy and Food Commissioner, " is sending out a Macedonian cry and pleading for our best friend, the dairy cow." He noted that the average Minnesota cow produced 81 pounds of butter annually 12 years ago; in 1902 the average was 166 pounds. There are now nearly one million cows in Minnesota and 679 creameries producing 75,000,000 pounds of butter annually, having the approximate value of $15,000,000. This was a gratifying showing; yet the Commissioner observed that Minnesota should eventually produce dairy products worth

$100,000,000, if her readily available sources were developed.

This pronounced movement in Minnesota for the attraction of labor and further development is scarcely less marked in the other Northern agricultural States, and it is noteworthy that the urged diversification of industries appeals particularly to the possible services of the immigrant Italian accustomed to intensive farming and peculiarly adaptable to the production of fruit and vegetables and dairy work.

To the South, also, the attraction of emigration from the Northern States to Canada is of serious consequence in its competition with Southern efforts to draw desirable settlers from the North. No other section of our country has been so slightly affected by foreign emigration. Most sharply is the contrast pointed in the " New York Sun " that, " in all the eleven States of the old Southern Confederacy there were in 1900 less than one-half as many foreign born as there were in the city of New York alone, and, of the number, more than one-half were in the single State of Texas, and even there the foreign born population was not six per cent. of the whole." Yet, no other part of our country is now so ardent in its appeal for settlers and no other is apparently so gravely in need of an influx of emigrant labor. The time has gone by when the South was too poor to advance its own development rapidly with outside capital. Its industries within the past decade have been flourishing as never before. Its rice crop increased from 115,000,000 pounds in 1898 to 400,000,000 pounds in 1903, and its cotton and tobacco crops have advanced to proportions beyond all anticipations. In 1893 the cotton crop of the United States was 6,717,142 bales. The cotton crop of 1903 was 10,727,-559 bales, marking an increase in 10 years of nearly two-thirds. The census report of 1900 shows an increase in the acreage of the tobacco crop in the preceding decade of 58.4 per cent. and an increased production of 77.8 per cent. Yet the demand in both cases has run far ahead of the supply.

Its manufacturing industrial enterprises and establishments have expanded even more phenomenally and, in every avenue, its effective capacity for production has far outstripped its available labor supply. This has been recognized for years past by the energetic managers of its railway lines and its more enterprising landowners, and remarkable efforts have been put forth for the attraction of settlement and the development of its resources. It is only within recent years, however, that the value to the South of the direct attraction of foreign emigration has been largely appreciated. The promotion of settlement from the native contribution from our Northern States was preferred and hundreds of inquiries recently addressed by me to leading landowners and the active managers of immigration and development associations marked the continuance of this preference.

It is now largely recognized, however, that it is hopeless to expect any adequate meeting of the demands from the South for labor from any available sources in other States of the Union. A determined resolution is manifest therefore to break down any lingering prejudice against foreign immigration and to promote its distribution through the South by organized effort. The possession of a certain amount of capital is no longer regarded as an almost indispensable requisite. For the poorest immigrant as well as for the established settler in the North the assurance of a welcome and a profitable opening are even now provided in many sections, and this attraction will soon be multiplied.

Already a most noteworthy recognition of the peculiar adaptability of the Italian to the labor conditions of the South has been accorded in Southern journals of foremost influence and standing. An authoritative attestation of his services in the Raleigh (N. C.) " Observer," November 6, 1904, is particularly comprehensive and pithy.

" ITALIAN IMMIGRATION IN THE SOUTH "

" Each year the labor problem grows more serious for the Southern farmer.

" The negro has always constituted the South's principal laboring contingent. But his increasing deficiency makes it necessary for additional help to be found. Without detracting from what is being done by the better class of negro workers, it is evident that the negro race cannot wholly meet in quantity or quality the demands for service that must be made on it for proper development of this great section of the country.

" In a small way, a number of experiments in other kinds of labor have recently been tried in Eastern North Carolina. Finns, Poles, Portuguese, Austro-Hungarians and Italians have all been introduced as laborers. The Italians have come in the largest numbers, and though often working under unfavorable conditions, have generally made satisfactory workers. In railroad building at Newbern, saw-milling at Dover, contract work at Kinston, fishing at Wilmington, oyster-canning at Beaufort and truck farming at various points, they have done so well that many are beginning to regard their judicious introduction here as the solution of the labor problem.

" In other sections of the South, where it has been extensively tried, Italian labor has proved itself well-nigh indispensable in the cultivation of the immense plantations. Notably in Louisiana, Alabama and Mississippi, it is an established fact that the Italian workman is sought for and appreciated, because he has demonstrated his worth as a laborer.

" Of the success of Italian immigration to Louisiana,

171

some idea may be gained from the following letter written last July by C. L. Buck, of Independence, La.:

" ' Twenty years ago land could be bought in and around the town for $1 to $5 per acre that is now selling readily at $25 to $100 per acre. One tract here of 1,500 acres sold twenty-five years ago for $1,600, and only a few weeks ago the purchaser sold 200 acres for $10,400. The assessed value of lands in this parish has been doubled in the past four years.

" ' One will ask what was the principal cause of the development. The answer must be the Italian immigration that has come here and improved the conditions in respect to production. The majority of farmers have done away with negro labor. Why? Because they are a shiftless, worthless sort, whereas the Italian laborer is a success. His sole object is to make money, and he knows it must come out of the ground; therefore, he is always at work when his work is needed.

" ' The question of his desirability as a citizen is often asked. I can say that thus far in our twelve or fifteen years' experience with them, they have given no trouble to any one. They are prompt to pay their debts at the stores, meet their paper at the banks when due, and often before. I do not think there is a case on record in this parish where the State has had to prosecute them for a crime or misdemeanor, and that is saying a great deal when we consider that there are 150 to 250 families living here, and every berry season there are probably 500 or more who come to assist in harvesting the crops.

" ' I can speak from experience, and say that thus far I have found them good neighbors and good tenants. They are frugal and industrious, and when working as tenants they are always willing to do their part, and I find it a great improvement and cheaper than the negro labor of to-day, that wants a dollar per day for a half dollar's worth of work. As tenants they never take up more at the store than will be realized from the crops, as is often the case with the negro.

" ' After they are here awhile they become more or less Americanized, and live better and spend more money as their means justify. They are, generally speaking, cleanly about their houses. They are capable of improvement in many ways, which is not the case with the negro; and as far as I know here, they have conducted themselves in a moral, law-abiding way. I am of course speaking of the past and present experience we have had with them.

" ' As fruit and truck growers they will be hard to beat, and I see no reason why they cannot be used to advantage for other sorts of farming. They soon make fair to good plough hands, though at first they are green about handling a horse.

" They are not hard to teach, as a rule. They want to make money, which is their sole object, and they try to follow instructions, and it is inevitable that if they make any, the landlord will, too. This immediate section would never have been what it is in so short a time without the Italian labor. The price of land is no object if they want it and can see their way clear to make a living on it. If they think they can make a living on 10 acres of land and have $1,000, they will try it, and not think it too much.

" ' They reason that it is that much invested from which they can derive a livelihood and have a home besides. Numbers of them have settled here on 10-acre plots and made a living and saved up money, notwithstanding the fact that the family was of large size. So far, we find them peaceful, law-abiding citizens without the dreaded stiletto. This is giving a general history of them as I know it. Of course, some are more prosperous than others. ' "

" In Mississippi thousands of Italians have been established in colonies, recently visited by Lee J. Langley, special correspondent of the ' Manufacturers' Record,' who says they already " ' Own their lands, are building their houses and becoming equal to every independent citizen of this country. ' "

From correspondence and press reports in hand the facts stated in the " Observer " appear to be beyond serious dispute. The following extract from a letter dated Nov. 14, 1904, addressed to Mr. John J. D. Trenor by Andrew Carnegie, in response to his inquiry, will be recognized as exceptionally authoritative:

Rising Demand for Italian Immigrant Labor

" As the result of experience, I rate the Italian highly and consider him a most desirable immigrant. It is to him I look with hope to settle more and more in our Southern States and finally to grow more cotton, which is already needed to supply the world's wants.

" As long as we can keep out the immigrants who are assisted to pay their passage, I think the danger from immigration largely imaginary.

" I want no better proof that a man is to be a valuable citizen than the fact that in Italy or in any European country he has succeeded in saving enough to bring himself and his family to the land of promise."

It may safely be anticipated that the demand for Italian labor in the South is certain to expand with the spreading knowledge of Italian character, industry and endurance. In view of the watchful guardianship of the Italian Emigration Department, however, and the imperative need of holding as well as attracting immigration, the promoters of settlement must operate with good judgment and treat the Italian immigrants with scrupulous fairness, or there will certainly be no influx to brag of. In the latest report of Adolfo Rossi, Chief Inspector of the Royal Emigration Department, this conclusion is emphasized in a way that should warn every State in our Union not to fail to protect the Italian in America from harsh treatment and greedy impositions.   ELIOT LORD.

CHAPTER IX

It must be clearly borne in mind that the existence of certain inconveniences or even evils now attending the flow of the current of immigration does not warrant, necessarily, the corrective of exclusion. The swollen current of a stream may overflow the limits of its bed, deluging the border lands with the spread of swamps, but this overflow does not prove that the flood is necessarily a burden on the surrounding country nor that a stoppage of the flow of water is the right prescription.

Along the Pacific slope vast stretches of barren ground are now blossoming and bearing fruit by the diversion of freshets into myriad channels of irrigation, and the hope of the arid plains beneath the Rocky Mountains chain is centred in the like distribution of the water now running to waste. Here it is patent to the dullest mind that the proper treatment of an enriching overflow is not to choke it off, but to divert it intelligently for the service of the land that needs it.

Can it be contended that the analogy is unfounded— that the flow of productive water is indeed a good thing for the country but the entry of productive labor is something to be dreaded and forbidden? Will this be maintained in view of the nation which has sprung from the loins of the immigrant and grown in greatness and prosperity so marvellously with the swelling tide of immigration in the last century?

Who will venture to question that a healthy, honest, willing laborer in any field of employment is an addition to the working capital and productive power of a nation? Has our growth reached the limit of expansion, or possible utilization of working capital and productive force? If not, why should we shun now what so many countries have vainly sought—the attraction to our shores of new workers to develop our resources? Little Belgium is not groaning under the burden of a population of producers fully twenty-five times as great as ours in proportion to the national territory, yet we hear querulous protests from time to time that our big country is overcrowded with laborers—that there is not work enough in sight to employ the hands already outstretched and that immigrants only come in to take away the jobs of our own workmen. If this country should be moved to confess that it is disposed to reject and exclude an influx of working capital because it sees no way to employ it and can devise none, it might study with profit the economy of New Zealand.

There the established Department of Labor, prac-

The Italian in America

tically in charge of its permanent head, Mr. Edward Tregear, has regarded as its first and chief duty—"its vital duty," he calls it—"the practical task of finding where labor was wanted and depositing there the labor running elsewhere to waste." . . . "The means employed by Mr. Tregear," as noted by Henry Demarest Lloyd, "are the maintenance of a widely extended system of agencies for bringing workers and work together, a strict decentralization of the unemployed by scattering them through the colony, and a refusal to give anything. Aid is furnished by sending the worker to private employment or, if to public works, only to such as were necessary and reproductive. . . . .

"Two features have characterized this policy from the beginning; the men were given nothing but a chance, and no work was made for the sake of making work. Nothing was undertaken that was not necessary and would not be profitable to the community. . . . The man had to pay ultimately for everything—for the railroad ticket taking him and his family to their new home, for the food and shelter they had on their way, for the tools he found ready for him, for the tents, for everything.

"The experience of New Zealand does not sustain the idea so prevalent that city people and artisans cannot make a living on the land. Some of the most successful settlers have been men brought up as tailors or shoemakers and workers in other trades in the city of London. Sailors and day laborers have been successful too."

It may be a novel function of government to undertake the distribution of labor, but it is none the less more rational than an edict of exclusion would be, or the tolerance of congestion and slums now is. If there is a conservative shrinking from the resolute grip of New Zealand in handling the labor problem as a national concern vitally affecting the public welfare, there should be, at least, no hesitation in according some co-operation with state, civic and individual organizations for the better distribution and utilization of the influx of working capital in the person of the immigrant.

Certainly our government might go as far as this, not only with entire propriety but without any straining of precedent. In the Act of 1864 expressly to encourage immigration, provision was made for the collection and dissemination of information in various languages to promote the choice and distribution of settlement. In presenting the bill then enacted, Senator Sherman said: " If official documents, prepared from official sources, could be furnished to foreigners desiring to come to this country, giving them accurate information as to the needs of labor in this country, there is no doubt that it would encourage a great deal of immigration." The expense of this provision, as Senator Sherman observed, would be practically inconsiderable in comparison with its certain benefit to the country. The misjudged repeal of this Act, in a fit of shortsighted economy four years later, prevented the proper development of its benefits but it did not contravene the sagacious judgment and foresight of Senator Sherman.

Objection to any such provision to-day on the score of expense would not be tenable for a moment in view of the rolling up of the " Immigrant Fund " through the institution and increase of the head-tax; as any outlay for this purpose would be wholly defrayed by the enforced contribution of the immigrants themselves for the oversight and regulation of their entry into this country. Even if it is no longer desired to encourage immigration, in view of the present influx, it would be none the less advisable to make some rational provision for the better distribution of the incoming labor seeking openings for employment in the development of the country.

Through the stretch of enactments for the prohibition of the entry of immigrants under contract, the transporting agencies have been debarred even from the circulation of ordinary guide books for immigrants, presenting accurately the industrial conditions here and the actual openings for settlement and employment. It is incontestable that the congestion so much complained of along the Atlantic seaboard has been largely due to the lack of correct information and channels of distribution that might readily be opened through a bureau of correspondence.

The Call for Better Distribution

If private and even State agencies cannot be trusted to prepare such information and open such channels, there can be no question of the right of Congress to make such provisions under its constitutional authorization to operate for the national welfare.

The call for this undertaking has been repeatedly emphasized by our Commissioners of Immigration, and is indeed expressly set forth in the latest reports of the present Commissioner General. The lack of this simple precaution for the avoidance and relief of congestion has been remarked with surprise for years by expert observers of the flow of immigration and its effects. Ten years ago, Edward Everett Hale made particular note of it in a contribution to "The Social Economist." "When Mr. George Jacob Holyoake was in this country some years ago, he called my attention to the absolute indifference of the general government to the great tide of foreign immigration. He said that the general government might, without much difficulty, provide a convenient manual which should tell the ignorant European where he wanted to go. If he wanted to raise wheat, it could direct him to a wheat country; if he wanted to raise oranges, it could direct him; if he wanted to skate or cut ice, it could instruct him as well."

Dr. Hale goes on to say that he has repeatedly but ineffectually sought to draw attention to this appeal. " The truth is," he observes pointedly, " that the wave of immigration has come without our asking for it; it has enriched us without our care, and speaking for organizations, whether of churches or of states, we have let it alone with a sublime indifference which would hardly be conceived possible if it were not everywhere apparent."

The only marked exception to this indifference to-day has been in the concentration of attention upon the filtering of the flow of immigration. We have enacted and enforced every rational precaution, and overstrained some to prevent the entry of objectionable immigrants and the importation of any by contract or, even, the assurance of employment; but the distribution and occupation of the checked and filtered flow have been almost utterly neglected as if they were of no concern to the national welfare.

The chief remedy for congestion proposed in bills before Congress is a further exclusion of immigration, by enacting a so-called "educational test" of desirability. An immigrant may be a skilled artisan; he may be an experienced farmer, honest, industrious, thrifty, able at once to contribute to the national productiveness and to rear a family of ambitious, patriotic young Americans—in the eye of common sense and reason a desirable settler —yet he will be barred out if he is unable to read from twenty to twenty-five words of the Constitution of the United States. A requirement, rational if applied to an applicant for the voting franchise, is irrationally imposed to restrict the opportunity of using a spade or an axe, or a pick in the development of this country and to debar the right of life, liberty and the pursuit of happiness here. Hundreds of thousands of illiterate immigrants have been pioneers of civilization here, piercing the pathless woods, opening the mines of ore and transforming the wastes to harvest lands. If the soil of America is to be reserved for scholars, Columbus should have been notified not to discover it with an illiterate crew.

In spite of the " illiterate " influx, the American standard of labor and living, broadly or nationally viewed, has been advancing persistently from decade to decade—as indisputable statistics prove. Until this demonstration of assimilation and progress can be upset by evidence that will bear examination, there is neither reason nor justice nor expediency in excluding honest, able-bodied men and women, who are seeking to escape from distressful conditions in the Old World, and denying them education, advancement, or even security for life.

The New South is already giving object lessons to the country at large in the successful attraction and utilization of the influx so heedlessly reckoned as " undesirable." The Four States Immigration League, composed of representatives of business organizations in Alabama, Louisiana, Mississippi and Texas, was chiefly incorporated for the purpose of devising ways and means for securing desirable immigrants for the several States represented.

" It was keenly realized," observed the Chattanooga " Times," in October, 1903, " that of the enormous inflow from the old country during the past twelve months, the number seeking homes in the South was ridiculously small and out of all proportion to the importance of the country and the inducements our productive fields hold out to home seekers."

In substantial recognition of this fact, an Immigration Bureau was established by the city of Chattanooga on its own account, and similar organizations in extension of the aims of the Four States League to other States have been perfected and are fast multiplying throughout the Southern States. South Carolina and several other States have now fully organized, active departments of agriculture and immigration, and the vigorous co-operation of all the leading railway lines has been certainly assured.

The peculiar adaptability of Italian immigrant labor to the requirements of the South has already been demonstrated beyond question, as noted in a preceding chapter, by many working and successful illustrations, and the South is fast awaking to the desirability of attracting the laborers of this nationality. They are more quickly inured to the climate than the immigrants from Northern Europe; they soon become adept in the cultivation of the crops of the South, and they have no rooted prejudice to competition with negro labor. Intermixture with negro labor can usually be obviated by the division of employment on plantations and any necessary association of the Italian whites with the blacks is not precluded by any race animosity.

The officials at Ellis Island, who are called upon to give counsel or directions to many thousands of immigrants yearly, have been pelted with letters during the past year from Southern railroads, real estate companies, and plantations asking for immigrant help. One railroad company alone gave notice that it wanted 10,000 families on its land, and would give away homesteads to any who would settle permanently along its lines. In the competition of these improvement associations for labor, a number of applicants deposited in New York banks special funds to be drawn upon to pay the travelling expenses of immigrants who were unable to pay their own expenses.

Advantage was taken of this pressure of application last year in the relief of distress in the detention rooms, when 21 immigrants, so poor that they would otherwise be liable to become public charges, were forwarded to an applicant at Memphis, Tennessee. The message accompanying this application was typical. " The families would be obliged to work with me one year in order to finish the cotton crop; otherwise it would be an entire loss to me: We cannot pick up hands every day. I consider this part of the United States (Clarkville, Miss.) the best for a poor man. If emigrants object to work side by side with negroes, I can say that is not necessary; each man has the land to himself and comes in contact with only the land-owner. I have no particular desire for any nationality, only parties that have been living on farms and are used to farm work. If I could be successful in this move, there could come more than 10,000 families and all find good homes. In case you can get any families, no matter how many at a time, send them on. The money for transportation is at the National Bank of Commerce for you to draw on as you need it."

The particular immigrants transported were of German nativity and sent on, after consultation, with the approval of the German Consulate in New York. There can be no question that Italian immigrants are soon likely to profit largely by this pressure from the South and the extension of its provisions for distribution and settlement. There can be no doubt, either, that intelligently directed efforts for the promotion of this supply of labor would meet a ready response from Italians already settled here in congested districts. It is by these and like means now certainly extending that the only really pressing problem of immigration, the betterment of distribution, is approaching its solution.

Thus far, however, there has been no substantial provision for any systematic, comprehensive and sustained distribution. The efforts to promote it are chiefly important in their demonstration of needs and openings and the assurance of co-operation, when it is resolutely under-

The Call for Better Distribution

taken, as it should be, by our national government. It is patently the view of the present Commissioner General of Immigration, that further delay in grappling with this problem is intolerable. In his latest report he enforces " the imperative, the immediately impending and rapidly augmenting necessity, both on the score of humanity and self-defence, of attempting a distribution of the ever inflowing tide of aliens."

He recognizes the call for distribution in " the millions of untilled acres and the unsatisfied demand for agricultural and other manual labor," but the main stress of his appeal for action is laid on the burdens and evils arising from the congestion of the influx. This undertaking may be properly tentative, at first, beginning, perhaps, with no more than bureaus of reliable information and the registration of applications for labor and employment in our principal ports of entry, but the extension of service may follow as rapidly as its evolution is justified by well-considered experiments.

The chief blocks in the way of success are likely to be the conservative questioning of any novel exercise of power by the national government, the jealousy and rivalry of States and districts competing for labor supply, the risk of conflict with labor unions, the ignorance and prejudice of the immigrants and the dread of the promotion of immigration by any effective provision for its distribution. The undertaking may be opposed, too, by those who measure the thrift and capacity of an immigrant by the extent of his cash in hand and set their faces stubbornly against "assisted immigration," in the teeth of the fact that a great proportion of the immigrants coming here during the last half century have been "assisted" covertly, if not openly, without any damage to this country comparable with the value of their labor, and the further fact that no statutory prohibition of "assistance" can possibly be enforced.

The extraordinary recent advance of Canadian population and industries carries a warning, too, that our national apathy in regard to immigration may no longer be continued with prudence. Canadian government and other agencies are now energetically encouraging, receiving and distributing immigration, as before noted, and making a mock of our dilatory and fumbling procedure. It surely behooves a nation that has grown great through immigration not to reverse its traditional policy of welcome, and resort to carping complaints and foolish bars as a confession of inability to grapple with any local perplexity of congestion.

The London "Saturday Review" has never been suspected of cherishing any disposition to over-rate America or Americans, but a recent issue of this critical journal contains a recognition which every patriotic American may well prize, and a forecast which only our incredible blundering in regard to immigration can falsify.

The Call for Better Distribution

"THE INDEPENDENCE OF THE UNITED STATES

" More than any other country of the present time, with the possible exception of the Russian Empire, the United States may be regarded as a complete, homogeneous, economic entity. It is able to grow all the corn it requires; it can raise all the live stock that it needs; its cotton plantations are sufficient to supply all its requirements; its mineral resources, both of base and precious metals, are extensive, and its coal mines are inexhaustible.

" Add to this every year enormous accessions by immigration of carefully selected, adult, able-bodied and skilled workmen to assist in the development of these very varied resources. The development of that country is probably due in large degree to these causes. The policy of protection, which it has extended to industries, has only hastened the natural and inevitable growth of the country. We may be sure that, in the future, it will become more and more independent of all other countries." *

                                        ELIOT LORD.

* Quotation of "The Saturday Review" in "The New York Sun," New York, October 19, 1904.

CHAPTER X

A cartoon appearing not long ago in one of our American city newspapers was a graphic exhibit of a popular fallacy. It represented a prodigious steamship stretching through the Mediterranean and across the Atlantic from Italy to New York. At the stern of this vessel, on the Italian coast, a mammoth poorhouse rose in view, from which a procession of paupers was pouring over the decks of the ship in unbroken ranks into another mammoth poorhouse on the American shore. In fervid colors also our country has often been painted as an abject dumping ground for beggars and cripples and criminals of every stripe—the spew of the slums of the Old World, voiding the lame, diseased and blind, evicted jail birds and notorious rascals, the burdens and pests of society, on our long-suffering Republic. One sample extract from a New York newspaper condenses this tirade.

" The floodgates are open. The bars are down. The sally-ports are unguarded. The dam is washed away. The sewer is unchoked. Europe is vomiting! In other words, the scum of immigration is viscerating upon our shores.

Pauperism, Disease and Crime

The horde of $9.60 steerage slime is being siphoned upon us from Continental mud tanks."

In view of the grossness of this misrepresentation, no serious rejoinder would be called for were it not for the possible impress of the persistence of this vituperation. Where there is so much smoke, it may be inferred, there must be some flame. The simple presentation of facts beyond contravention will suffice to show how grotesquely the truth has been distorted.

The gigantic poorhouse or system of poorhouses of the American bugbear does not exist in Italy. There is no poor law in the kingdom, and no one has a legal claim for maintenance at the expense of the State unless he be infirm, insane or an infant. There are many charitable foundations endowed by private beneficence, but there are comparatively few asylums for the poor. A certain amount of begging is allowed, and there are still, no doubt, many beggars in Italy, especially in the Southern Provinces—but there are few beggars among the sturdy laborers who have the enterprise and the will to seek for work in a country so distant and intolerant of drones. Our restrictive immigration laws, moreover, specifically exclude professional beggars, paupers and persons likely to become a public charge, as well as all idiots, lunatics, epileptics, persons afflicted with a loathsome or dangerous contagious disease, persons convicted of a felony or other crime or misdemeanor involving moral turpitude, prostitutes, polygamists and anarchists. The official papers, which every immigrant to this country from Italy must procure, and the strict examination here, practically bar the entry of any considerable number of the classes now justly excluded by law. No current misapprehension nor calumny can rebut this conclusion.

This is pithily affirmed in the official report of the United States Commisioner General of Immigration for the year 1895-96, for example: " It is gratifying to me to be again able to report to you that I know of no immigrant landed in this country within the last year who is now a burden upon any public or private institution.

" With some exceptions, the physical characteristics of the year's immigration were that of a hardy, sound, laboring class, accustomed and apparently well able to earn a livelihood wherever capable and industrious labor can secure employment."

If Italian beggars were to be found anywhere in this country they would be proportionately most numerous in Greater New York, for the mass of immigrants land here, usually with only a few dollars in their pockets, and their poverty has greatly retarded their spreading throughout the country. Yet, even in this most trying situation, the Italian can point with pride to the records of his comparative standing.

On common beggary in New York City, Jacob Riis writes with conceded authority in " How the Other Half

Pauperism, Disease and Crime

Lives ": " It is curious to find preconceived notions quite upset in a review of the nationalities that go to make up this squad of street beggars. The Irish lead the list with fifteen per cent., and the native American is only a little way behind with twelve per cent., while the Italian has less than two per cent. Eight per cent. were Germans. The relative prevalence of the races in our population does not account for this showing. Various causes operate, no doubt, to produce it. Chief among them is, I think, the tenement itself. It has no power to corrupt the Italian, who comes here in almost every instance to work. No beggars would ever emigrate from anywhere unless forced to do so."

Another authoritative record giving an exact exhibit of pauperism in New York City and its distribution by nationalities is presented in the Thirty-fifth Annual Report of the State Board of Charities of New York, containing the proceedings of the New York State Conference of Charities and Correction at the Second Annual Session held in New York City, November 19, 20, 21 and 22, 1901. At this Conference an address on " The Problems of the Almshouse " was given by Hon. John W. Keller, President of the Department of Public Charities of the City of New York. He defined the almshouse referred to in his discussion as follows: " In the Boroughs of Manhattan and the Bronx, the Almshouse is that group of buildings on Blackwell's Island where the helpless and friendless, destitute citizens of these two Boroughs are cared for at the public expense. In the Borough of Brooklyn there is a similar institution at Flatbush, and in the Borough there is a Poor Farm." In the course of his discussion the following tables were presented:

Table " A " (showing the nativity of persons admitted to the Almshouse in 1900):

	Male.	Female.	Total.
United States....................	355	199	554
Ireland	808	809	1,617
England and Wales..............	111	87	198
Scotland	25	14	39
France	19	2	21
Germany..........................	290	84	374
Norway, Sweden and Denmark....	22	6	28
Italy	15	4	19
Other countries...................	50	36	86
Total........................	1,695	1,241	2,936

" Out of a total of 2,936 only 554 were born in the United States; 2,382 were foreign-born, and of this number 1,617 were born in Ireland alone."

Table " B " (showing nativity of those admitted to the Incurable Hospital during the year 1900):

	Male.	Female.	Total.
United States....................	7	4	11
Ireland	5	6	11
England	1	1	2
Poland	..	1	1
Germany	4	..	4
Italy	..	1	1
Total........................	17	13	30

Pauperism, Disease and Crime

Table " C " (showing nativity of those admitted to the Blind Asylum during the year 1900):

	Male.	Female.	Total.
United States......................	45	4	49
Ireland	36	3	39
England	3	..	3
Germany	4	1	5
Italy	1	..	1
Total........................	89	8	97

Another equally conclusive exhibit is furnished from Boston, which comes next to New York in its receipts of immigration, in the Twenty-third Annual Report of the Associated Charities of Boston, November, 1902.

" The variation in the number of Italians applying for assistance is interesting. Fifty-four families came to us in 1891, and only 69 in the last year, though the Italian population of this city has in the meantime increased from 4,718 to 13,738. This fact seems to corroborate the report of Conference 6 (embracing the North-End District or Italian quarter) which describes the Italian immigrant as usually able to get on by himself except in case of sickness, when temporary help is needed."

It is obvious that this report marks not only a low rate of pauperism but a very material decrease in the percentage of applicants for charity in the face of the often maligned influx during the closing years of the last century.

The Italian in America

The report of District 6 Conference, referred to in the above summary, remarks, " as the Italian families so largely outnumber the others, and as the Italian element is now predominant in the district, it is worth while to note the chief causes of extreme poverty.

" We observe that intemperance is not found as a chief or as a subsidiary cause in any of this year's list of Italian families. Sickness was the leading chief cause (10) and also the leading subsidiary cause (9); next in order come the following chief causes: lack of employment due to no fault of the employee (4); physical or mental defects (2); roving disposition (3); dishonesty (2); disregard of family ties, lack of training for work, and lack of thrift (1 each).

" If any general inference is fair from so small a number of cases, it is that the Italian families referred to us have not been in the greatest distress. The majority of the Italians are apparently fairly thrifty and those who have trouble are often helped by their countrymen. The little that we have been called upon to do has in some cases set a family at once upon their feet."

The assumption that illiteracy is a prolific source of pauperism is not sustained by the examination of cases known to this conference, so far, at least, as the Italian immigrant is concerned. " In the matter of illiteracy," the Conference of District 6 states, " we can give positive information about only 45 of the 68 families (applying for aid)—mostly Italians." The record shows 32

Italian families, with 64 parents born in Italy. " Among heads of these families, we find 32 who can read and write; 2 who can read and not write, while 11 can neither read nor write."

As to the burden imposed by recent arrivals the report of Conference 4 is noteworthy. " We found that none of the new arrivals (needing help) were recent immigrants, and that almost all of the parents were born in the United States or Great Britain."

These particular conclusions are roundly sustained and confirmed by the determination of the general distribution of pauperism by nationalities in the Report of the United States Industrial Commission on Immigration transmitted to the Fifty-seventh Congress. " The proportion of the different nationalities among the paupers in our almshouses varies very greatly. The Irish show far and away the largest proportion, no less than 7,550 per million inhabitants, as compared with 3,031 for the average of all the foreign born. The French come next, while the proportion of paupers among the Germans is somewhat unexpectedly high. The remarkably low degree of pauperism among the Italians is possibly due to the fact that such a large percentage of them are capable of active labor, coming to this country especially for that purpose."

These conclusions are further substantiated by the report of the Commissioner General of Immigration for the fiscal year ending June 30, 1904, in which statistics are presented as to aliens detained in the charitable institutions in the United States. It appears that excluding the insane, there were at the time of this examination 15,396 aliens in the charitable institutions of the United States. In the division by races, the Irish and Germans largely exceed the Italians, there being 4,599 Irish, 2,949 Germans, 1,230 Italians and 1,309 English.

Passing to the insane, the enumeration shows a still greater disparity, namely, 5,943 Irish; 4,808 Germans; 1,822 English; 1,985 Scandinavians, and 718 Italians.

As shown by the analysis of the Bureau of Immigration, the proportion of Irish in the charitable institutions is 30 per cent., of Germans, 19 per cent., of English, $8\frac{5}{10}$ per cent., while the Hebrews and Italians are both 8 per cent.

DISEASE

The high average physical vigor of the immigrants from Italy is demonstrated by their endurance of the most exhausting labors under trying climatic conditions. It is questionable whether the immigrants from any other country show an equal adaptation to the rigors of our Northern winters and the intense sun glare on our Southern plantations. The endurance of climatic shifts and extremes without distress is in a measure accounted for by the fact that so many have been inured to such conditions in their own country, for in spite of their nearer approach to the tropics, the mountainous districts of Italy are often colder in winter than any considerable district in England. Moreover, there is less provision, ordinarily, in Italy for the artificial heating of houses in winter and Italians live without a shiver in cold rooms which the average Englishman or American would not tolerate.

All reliable statistics of disease and mortality obtainable here show that the Italians, as a body, are so healthy and rugged that their death rate is comparatively low ordinarily, and that they are remarkably free from disease outside of the congested centres. The power of resistance to disease is impaired in children born in unsanitary quarters, but this is rather a reproach to the inadequacy of tenement house regulation than to the degeneracy of the stock. The exact reports obtainable in Boston may fairly be taken as an exhibit of the average in American cities. In a communication to *Charities*, May 7, 1904, Rocco Brindisi, M.D., summarizes the comparison of mortality in this city for a typical year. "In 1902 there were in Boston 641 deaths among the Italians. Of the deceased, 175 were born in Italy and 466 were born in America of Italian parents. The total figures represent 6 per cent. of the total number of deaths in the city of Boston and 11.43 per thousand of the population. This rate of mortality is lower than that of any other nationality except the Russians."

It is noted by the same authority that the largest percentage of sickness is furnished by the newcomers, as might naturally be expected, and by the women and children. The newly arrived immigrants, especially when they land in the early spring, " pay their tribute to acclimation by contracting rheumatic and respiratory diseases, such as rheumatism, bronchitis, pneumonia, pleuritis." Yet the vigor of these immigrants is such, as he observes, that " the proportion of deaths is moderate, owing to the strong constitution, the youth and the temperate habits of the patients."

" The Italian women here are forced to change entirely their mode of living. From the active natural life in the open air they are plunged at once into a life of relative inactivity and seclusion, and consequently become more or less liable to general impairment of the organic functions. They are frequently affected with dysmenorrhea, dyspepsia, anemia, chlorosis and kindred diseases; and their impaired physical condition has an injurious effect on the children, who contribute largely to the mortality.

" Besides the maternal influence, improper nursing and insufficiency of fresh air are responsible for the great number of ailments and deaths among the Italian children. Rickets and tuberculosis are the most frequent general diseases. Bronchitis, broncho-pneumonia and pneumonia usually affect them in winter and intermediate seasons, while in the hot weather the dreadful host of the so-called summer complaints, from the irritative gastroenteritis to the deadly cholera infantum storms and ravages the Italo-American breed."

The congested conditions of living in the chief American cities are unquestionably responsible for the deplorable increase in sickness and mortality, and a better distribution is certainly the only remedy that will cut away the root of the complaint. The alleged low standard of living and improper diet of the Italians have also been held responsible by some observers. Mr. Robert A. Woods, of the well known Boston social establishment, the "West End House," characterizes their diet as "over-stimulating and innutritious." My own wide ranging observations do not support this conclusion. The Italian in our Northern States eats much more meat than he did in Italy, both because he can better afford to pay for it and likes it, and because he apparently feels the need of it in sustaining his fatiguing labors through our long, cold winter seasons. Other immigrants do likewise in the teeth of the protests of vegetarians, and the Italian does not appear to suffer from the change more than any other laboring man. Doubtless the reduction in the amount of meat and the increase of vegetables may be beneficial in many cases of Italians suffering from stomach troubles, as Dr. Brindisi observes, but this is a concern which advancing experience and instruction may be trusted to deal with. There is no substantial reason to maintain that the ordinary fare of the Italian workingman here is any more innutritious than that of any other laborer in a like situation, and there is substantial evidence that it is better cooked by the average housewife than in the families of workingmen generally. Moreover, the introduction of a variety of wholesome greens, celeries, dandelions, spinach, fennels, has been very greatly advanced throughout this country by Italian-American example and influence. The increased consumption of fruits in answer to the Italian demand and by the multiplication of fruit venders has been one of the most noteworthy accompaniments of the Italian immigration. "The Italians have in fact," observes the publication of the "South End House," "Americans in Process," "created a wholesome appetite for fruit among the mass of the people."

It is doubtless true, as Dr. Antonio Stella remarks, that the prevalence of consumption among the Italian population of our chief cities is distressful and even alarming, and that statistics arranged in accordance with the infection rate rather than the death rate would demonstrate this clearly, and I have not even the faintest desire to minimize the evil effects of congestion. But it is none the less true that the mortality rate in all these cities has fallen materially since the great influx in the last decade compelled public recognition of the crying need of better sanitation. The housing and general living conditions are officially certified to be better to-day than they were ten years ago, and improvement is steadily advancing. The

Pauperism, Disease and Crime

Italian share in this gain is unquestionable. Dr. S. H. Durgin, Chairman of the Boston Board of Health, gives evidence directly in point. " In a general way," he writes to Dr. Brindisi, " I would say that while the Italians are prone to over-crowding, they are in other respects found to be in a fair sanitary condition, and decidedly improving from year to year in our city."

Remedial measures to check the start and spread of disease in congested centres are still to be devised and extended, but there is on the whole no warrant for any alarmist view of Italian degeneracy in America. There is certainly no inherent lack of vitality in the people. On the contrary, as Dr. Stella observes, the Italians, except for this susceptibility to pulmonary disease, show the most wonderful elements of resistance and recuperation, as may be seen in the favorable manner they react to surgical operations, extreme temperatures and all sorts of trials.

THE IMMIGRANT AND CRIME

In view of the services of the immigrant in upbuilding this country, there might be some just palliation of a percentage of law-breaking in excess of that of the native born. The immigrant has not been reared in conformity with our laws and social restrictions, and has often been negligently housed in slums intolerable under proper sanitary and building regulations. Yet in spite of our slum traps it does not appear that the record of the foreign

born at large needs any special consideration. Hastings
H. Hart, General Secretary of the National Conference
of Charities and Correction, contributed a notable examination of the comparative criminality of our foreign and
native born population, in a communication to the " American Journal of Sociology " for November, 1896.

A common error arises, as he notes, " from comparing
the criminal population, foreign and native, with the
whole of the general population, foreign and native. The
young children of the community furnish practically no
prisoners and nearly all of these children are native born,
whether the parents are native born or not."

" Of the prisoners of the United States, 98.5 per cent.
are above the age of sixteen years; 95 per cent. are above
the age of eighteen years; and 84 per cent. are above the
age of twenty-one years. The native born population of
the United States in 1890 numbered 53,390,600; the
native born prisoners, 65,977; ratio 1,235 in a million.
The foreign born population numbered 9,231,381; the
foreign born prisoners, 16,352; ratio, 1,744 in a million;
an apparent excess of foreigners over natives of 41 per
cent. But the number of native born males of voting age
was 12,591,852; native born male prisoners, 61,637; ratio,
4,895 in a million. The number of foreign born males of
voting age was 4,348,459; foreign born male prisoners,
14,287; ratio, 3,285; showing an equal excess of natives
over foreigners of 50 per cent."

Pauperism, Disease and Crime

The basis of Mr. Hart's reckoning of parentage is criticized in the statistical report of the United States Industrial Commission on Immigration transmitted to Congress on December 5, 1901, but his general conclusion is affirmed as follows, viz.: " From this table it will be seen that taking the United States as a whole, the whites of foreign birth are a trifle less criminal than the total number of whites of native birth."

In the report of this Commission there is further noted the nationality which has contributed far more largely than any other to raise the average of the criminality and pauperism of the foreign born. " Taking the inmates of all penal and charitable institutions, we find that the highest ratio is shown by the Irish, whose proportion is more than double the average for the foreign born, amounting to no less than 16,624 to the million."

The comparative percentage of the criminality of Italians in this country is set high in this table, coming between the French and the Swiss, but the substantial accuracy of this rating is vitiated by the fact that the proportion of males and the comparative ages of the immigrants of the several nationalities do not enter into the reckoning. These elements are essential to any just and accurate determination of comparative criminality. It is only fair, too, to take into consideration the distribution of the nationalities. The rate of criminality is higher in city slums than amid the better surroundings of the country places at large. This abnormal criminality is unfairly charged against the people of the slum quarters, and there has been a strenuous harping on the disastrous effect of immigration in filling the slums of our cities and in the prolific breeding of crime and disease. Fortunately for the credit of the immigrants, there has been of late years a dawning perception that it is the tenement, not the tenant, that makes the slum, and that the rational remedy for congestion does not lie in the exclusion of the flow of productive labor but in its effective regulation and distribution. Our present slums are the natural outgrowth of the reckless laxity of our building laws and sanitary regulations. They are plainly chargeable to our civic blindness and the toleration of greed. It is the native-born rookery, not the foreign-born influx, that must bear the burden of reproach for the slum.

This has been conclusively demonstrated in the partial transformation already effected by the pressure of necessity and the sense of responsibility.

In the pithy conclusion of Jacob Riis, " wherever the Gospel and the sunlight go hand in hand in the battle with the slums, there it is already won—there is an end of it at once." Sometimes the slum has been conquered by cutting out sections bodily, as was done in the annihilation of the infamous Five Points, in the opening of Paradise Park, a playground for the children. "Mulberry

Pauperism, Disease and Crime

Bend," as Mr. Riis observes, "was the worst pigsty of all. I do not believe that there was a week in all the twenty years I had to do with the den as a police reporter, in which I was not called to record there a stabbing or shooting affair, some act of violence. It is now five years since the Bend became a Park, and the police reporter has not had business there once during that time; not once has a shot been fired or a knife been drawn. That is what it means to let the sunlight in and give the boys their rights in a slum like that." Or the slum has been overcome no less effectively by the reconstruction of tenements as was done by such builders as Miss Ellen Collins, who, in the words of Jacob Riis, " planted homes in the true sense of the word, in the very slum of slums, down in Water Street, ... right in the very devil's preserves, and beat him out of sight. . . . . The Water Street houses had been a veritable hell before she took hold there. The dark halls were a favorite hiding place for criminals when chased by the police. . . . . The buildings were unspeakably filthy, the saloon on the ground floor had finally been closed, after one of the bloody fights that were the rule of the neighborhood. Yet practically the same tenants are there to-day and have been there these twenty years. It was the landlord who has changed and furnished opportunities for the tenants to come up to. Miss Collins brought back the home, and her houses became good and decent; the whole neighborhood took a turn for the better, tried to come up to the ideal that she set before it."

Even less radical changes are very notably effective in the purification of the slum. "Even as I am writing," says Mr. Riis, "a transformation is being worked in some of the filthiest streets in the East Side by a combination of new asphalt pavements with a greatly improved street-cleaning service that promises great things. Some of the worst streets have, within a few weeks, become as clean as I have not seem them in twenty years and as they prob-ably never were since they were made. The unwonted brightness of the surroundings is already visibly reflected in the person and dress of the tenants, notably the chil-dren. They take to it gladly, giving the lie to the old assertion that they are pigs and would rather live like pigs."

Reconstruction is not a gift enterprise or charitable donation. Street widenings and the opening of squares and little parks are the changing of antiquated inconven-ient and unhealthy conditions for the essential require-ments of a modern city. Reconstruction of dwellings to meet proper requirements is not any half way approach to the erection of almshouses. It has been demonstrated over and over again that the so-called model tenements will unfailingly pay even higher average returns than the business buildings erected under modern regulations in the best city locations. Even where there is an apparent strain of philanthropy or extraordinary accommodation for the rental charges, as in the erection of the Riverside Tenements in Brooklyn, the return is certified to be never less than six and even seven per cent. on the investment. The landlord of these tenements, as Mr. Riis writes, " says with scorn that ' talk about the tenants coming up to their opportunities ' was the veriest humbug. They are there now, a long way ahead of the landlord." Here the central yard is a garden with flowers and a band-stand where a band plays sometimes at the landlord's expense; so, contrary to the common experience, " it is much better to live in the rear of the yard than in front."

Even under present conditions, the true effect of immigration on the slum is expertly marked by Jacob Riis: " It is nevertheless true that while immigration peoples our slums, it also keeps them from stagnation. The working of the strong instinct to better themselves that brought the crowds here forces layer after layer of this population up to make room for the new crowds coming in at the bottom, and thus a circulation is kept up that does more than any sanitary law to render the slums harmless. Even the useless sediment is kept from rotting by being constantly stirred."

A careful examination of police reports, secured from every city in this country, where nationalities are distinguished in the records of arrests, does not justify the assumption that the criminal tendencies of the Italians

The Italian in America

exceed the average of the foreign born or of the native population. It must be borne in mind that no comparison is valid which does not take into account the relative proportion of males and females and the factor of age. Yet in Boston, Providence and other cities, attracting the greater part of the Italian immigration to New England, the percentage of arrests of Italians is less than their percentage of the foreign born total. Two examples of this record may suffice:

	Boston.	Providence.
Total foreign born, Census 1900	197,129	55,855
Total born in Italy, Census 1900.........	13,738	6,252
Italian percentage of total foreign born...	7.0	11.2
Total arrests, foreign born	19,952	3,902
Total arrests, Italian nativity...........	1,219 (1903)	422 (1903)
Percentage of arrests...................	6.1	10.8

It will be noted that in both cases cited, the record of arrests is for 1903, three years later than the census count of population. Within these three years the Italian influx has raised materially the Italian percentage of the total foreign born; hence the strictly correct comparison would be more notably to the advantage of the Italians. In Paterson and other cities of New Jersey containing a considerable Italian population, the comparison of percentage is still more favorable to the Italian proportion of the foreign born. The comparison in New York City is slightly to the disadvantage of the Italians.

Pauperism, Disease and Crime

	New York.
Total foreign born, Census 1900	1,270,080
Total born in Italy, Census 1900........	145,433
Italian percentage of total foreign born.	11.5
Total arrests, foreign born.............	59,077
Total arrests, Italian nativity	7,307 (1900)
Percentage of arrests...................	12.3

But the annual influx is here so great that the census
count is considerably under the correct enumeration for
the full year 1900, the basis of the reckoning of percentage. Moreover, the record of arrests is scarcely even an
approximate measure of criminality. There is at the outset a deduction for discharges and acquittals for which
there are no special records showing distinction of nationalities. Then the arrests are largely for breaches of city
ordinances such as peddling without a license, which are
not criminal offences. The more recent immigrants like
the Italians are the most likely to break ordinances ignor-
antly and they are also most liable to suffer from hazing
and blackmailing impositions.

A more notable than creditable attempt has been made
to figure out an excess of Italian criminality above the
average by the singular device of dropping from the
record all crimes arising from drunkenness. This alleged
prop of immigration restriction was readily shaken in a
hearing given by the Senate Committee on Immigration
on December 9, 1902. " The Italian people," as I then
observed in briefly addressing the committee, " as a whole

are a frugal and industrious people. In our statistics we sometimes make discriminations against them that are not correct. We had an illustration of this in Massachusetts. A report was prepared by the Immigration Restriction League which was based upon the criminal record of the Italians in Massachusetts, leaving out all crimes which had been produced through intoxication. That is the way that ingenious plan of statistics was drawn. So they tried to make out a bad case against the Italians."

" Now Massachusetts is the one State in the Union that has made the most thorough examination of the whole question of the relation of intemperance to crime, and the report on that subject in 1895 by the Bureau of Labor Statistics there shows that about 87 per cent. of all the crime in Massachusetts grew out of intemperance in some form. When you take then the Italian population of Boston and of Massachusetts, and ask how many of these people were imprisoned or arrested or committed crime because of intemperance, you find that they rise away above all the Northern races. The Italian people are a temperate people, and while, in Massachusetts, three in a hundred of the Northern races, including the Scotch, the Irish, the English and the Germans were arrested for intemperance, only three in a thousand of the Italians were arrested. What a remarkable bearing that has upon desirability and availability! "

This evidence is further specifically attested in the report of the United States Industrial Commission on Immigration covering the tables compiled by the Prison Commissioners of Massachusetts. This report states: " It appears from the table that prisoners committed to all institutions in proportion to a thousand population of the same nativity indicates that those born in Massachusetts numbered 7.3 per thousand, but that, omitting those committed for intoxication the number is 2.6 per thousand. Below this proportion stand immigrants from Portugal, Austria, Germany, Russia and Finland. The leading nationality above this average is that of the Irish, whose commitments per thousand were 27.1, but omitting intoxication was 6. Next in order of commitments are Welsh, English, Scotch and Norwegians, all of which show a large predominance of intoxication. The Italians are a marked exception, the commitments numbering 12.9 for all causes, and 10 for causes except intoxication." In view of the very high proportion of males above the age of 18 in the Italian immigration, this record does not certainly appear to the disadvantage of the Italians. Their comparative temperance is further attested beyond question by the investigation made by the Committee of Fifty of nearly thirty thousand cases in the records of organized charity. Here intemperance was shown to be the principal cause of distress in twenty per cent. of the German cases, twenty-four per cent. of the American cases, twenty-five per cent. of the English cases and thirty-eight per cent. of the Irish cases; but in only three and one-half per cent. of the Italian cases.

An interesting typical exhibit of this distinguishing intemperance is contributed by Dr. Rocco Brindisi to "Charities." "Of the eighty-eight who died in Boston of alcoholism in the year 1902, none were Italian. During March (1904) 59 Italians were arrested by the police of Division I, which is in the heart of the Italian quarter (in Boston), and of these only 9 were for drunkenness. It is worthy of note that 5 were arrested on the eighteenth, that is, between St. Patrick's Day and St. Joseph's, which shows that they are not habitual drunkards, but go on a spree on holidays. Lieutenant Rosallo, to whom I am indebted for the above information, states that during his long service of seventeen years at the station, not one Italian woman was arrested for drunkenness."

The records in the smaller cities and country districts are less exact, but my personal inquiries and correspondence with observers throughout the country, assure the conclusion that crime among the Italians is comparatively rare in such locations. Schenectady may be taken as typical of the progressive manufacturing cities attracting Italian settlement in the East. Here, Mayor Eisenmenger, who served for many years as Justice of the Police Court, attests positively the general good conduct and character of the Italian workers in the city. The year 1893 was one of peculiar hardship, and he thought it really of special note that no Italian applied for public charity during that year, and no one was brought before his court for any serious offence. The canvass made by the " Manufacturers' Record " of the condition and progress of Italian plantation workers in the South obtained reports of a rarity of crime and even of misdemeanors that was very highly creditable to these immigrants.

There is a certain lack of reliable statistics showing comparative criminality, taking into consideration the essential elements of sex and age, but my personal investigation in all American cities containing a considerable Italian population leads to the conclusion that the proportion of crimes against the person is somewhat greater among the Italian population here than among natives, but the proportion of all crimes to the population is less. Furthermore, the testimony is general that affrays in which knives and pistols are used by Italians are in the great majority of instances confined to their own nationality. These grow largely out of jealous defence of wives, sisters, daughters or sweethearts, or resentment of rivalry. Often the inciting cause is covered by trivial pretences and a quarrel flames up for no reason apparent to ordinary observers.

There are, no doubt, too, murders of sheer brutality or those committed in the course of robbery. There are known instances also of blackmail and dastardly assassination by individuals or bands of ruffians. But such out-

The Italian in America

rages are utterly at variance with the known disposition of the great mass of the Italians in this country. There are vile men in every nationality, and it does not appear by any substantial evidence that the Italian is peculiarly burdened, though it has been unwarrantably reproached through ignorance or prejudice. This discrimination has doubtless arisen largely from the fact that crimes committed by the Italians are of a more sensational character than the average or are more readily inflated into popular sensations. Hence they are expanded in print under headlines that catch the eye and make an impress out of proportion to their comparative number.

Jacob Riis, one of the most keen and impartial of observers, sums up pithily his view of the offences of the Italian in America:

"With all his conspicuous faults, the swarthy Italian immigrant has big redeeming traits. He is as honest as he is hot-headed. There are no Italian burglars in the Rogues' Gallery; the 'ex-brigand' toils peacefully with pick-axe and shovel on American ground. His boy occasionally shows, as a pickpocket, the results of his training with the toughs of the Sixth Ward slums. The only criminal business to which the father occasionally lends his hand, outside of murder, is a bunco game, of which his confiding countrymen, returning with their hoard to their native land, are the victims. The women are faithful wives and devoted mothers. Their vivid and picturesque costumes lend a tinge of color to the otherwise dull monotony of the slums they inhabit. The Italian is gay, light-hearted, and, if his fur is not stroked the wrong way, inoffensive as a child. His worst offence is that he keeps the stale beer dives."

In the reports of the Industrial Commission on Immigration (Volume 15, page 480), 1901, it is observed that the crime rate of Italians chiefly on the score of crimes of violence is high in their own country. It is remarked, however, " there is reason to believe that conditions there are changing for the better, which will cause a corresponding change in the character of future immigration. It has been claimed, and statistics are given to substantiate the claim, that the part of the crime rate due to homicide is diminishing regularly and continuously in Italy, owing to the general extension of the influences of civilization, such as education, development of commerce, transportation, communication by newspapers, mail and telegraph. It is said, too, that emigration is helping in this process by, first, the greater prosperity brought to the country through returning emigrants, and, more powerfully by the more enlightened ideas brought back by them.

" As the Italian population increases here, moreover, the percentage of females and children increases, and this also will reduce their crime rate."

It has been estimated by an observant member of the

New York Prison Association that seventy-five per cent. of all crimes committed by Italians in this country are punished because of their open character, while seventy-five per cent. of all crimes in the United States go unpunished. If this calculation is reasonably correct, it would appear that the Italian is already receiving his full share of denunciation, restraint and punishment for his misdeeds in America.

There is no thought, of course, in this observation of suggesting any stretch of tolerance for the crimes committed by any Italians in this country. In fact the great mass of their own countrymen would be instantly resentful of any such plea or procedure. Their leading members in meetings of the Italian Chambers of Commerce and other representative associations have repeatedly appealed for the most active and vigorous enforcement of the laws to detect and punish blackmailers and other criminals who harass their peaceable and hard-working communities.

The apparent incapacity or ineffectiveness of the regular police force in districts where blackmailing has been most frequent and oppressive, is a deficiency that calls sharply for reform. In the weariness of waiting for proper official protection, it is not to be wondered at that Italians in some of our anthracite coal mining districts, especially, have been driven in self-defence to organize for their needed protection such vigilance committees as the St. Joseph Protective Association in Carbondale, Pa., and the like in Old Forge, Edgerton and smaller hamlets. The practical service of these self-defending associations is already obvious in the repression of blackmailing, but the terrorism in these districts still calls for redoubled energy on the part of the police and the adoption of every feasible restraint.

An admirable object lesson to every community plagued by blackmailers is offered in the method devised last year by Commissioner McAdoo in New York City for the detection and arrest of blackmailers and criminals of every stripe in the Italian quarters of Greater New York. This was the organization of a special "Italian Department" of his detective force headed by one of the most competent members of his staff, Detective Sergeant Petrosini. This force of twenty-nine members is made up of alert, keen and trustworthy men of Italian descent, thoroughly familiar with the Italian quarters and quick to scent out and pounce upon the rascals that have been infesting these quarters and furnishing the newspapers with visions of an imported Mafia.

The Commissioner states his disbelief in the transplanting of any such bogy organization, but he has rightly determined to stamp out the blackmailing pest in every guise in which it appears. He reports a gratifying reduction in this and other crimes in the Italian quarters through the persistent and expert services of this new

The Italian in America

department. It has already made many arrests, secured certain convictions, and driven numbers of criminals back to their native land where they will not escape surveillance and punishment, for their description and records are promptly furnished to the Italian police departments.

No measure of the Commissioner's administration has been better conceived and more signally successful. For the benefit of the Italians in New York and the country at large, it is only to be regretted that this device was not applied years ago, for it is clearly the one most needful and effective. Under the unbending requirements of the Civil Service examinations, no special openings can be made for Italians to enter the regular police force of the city, though more could, no doubt, be employed to advantage in the Italian quarters, but Commissioner McAdoo reports an evident ambition of so many young men of Italian descent to enter the service that the lack of policemen thoroughly familiar with these quarters will be supplied within a few years. The Italians in the city as elsewhere, are quick to respond to impartial and sympathetic treatment, and the conviction is now widespread that the head of the Police Department will treat one and all with scrupulous fairness of intention. There will be no occasion to worry over any peculiar exhibit of crime among the Italians in America if the common-sense restraint applied by Commissioner McAdoo is adopted or adapted wherever needed by an official in whom the mass of Italians have confidence.   SAMUEL J. BARROWS.

CHAPTER XI

It is a plainly untenable ground of objection to the entry of the Italian immigrant into this country that he has been reared under social and political institutions that clash with our republican principles. May not the like be urged against the admission of immigrants from almost every country in Europe? Why should this fact be more a disqualification to the Italian than to the German or Englishman or Irishman? Is he more backward than the immigrant of any other nationality in hearty appreciation of our free institutions and in the loyalty of his citizenship? On the contrary, it might rather be urged in his favor that no immigrant of any country excels him in the fervor of his appreciation of the free thought, free press, free school and free government of America.

The hatred of slavery has been an ever-burning passion in his bosom, even when inured to subjection by centuries of oppression. In the years before our war for the Union, Irving, Cooper and Longfellow had many admiring readers in Italy, but no other American book of that period or since has ever moved Italy like "Uncle Tom's Cabin."

The Italian in America

Throughout the darkest days of our Civil War the leading newspapers of North Italy, where alone the expression of opinion was free, were steadfast friends of the American North as the upholder of Liberty and Union, one and inseparable. For a like ideal, not many years after, dissevered and discordant Italy suppressed her feuds and jealousies, and the patriotic rising of her people broke every bond that fettered her aspiration.

Is the marking of class divisions or distinctions of rank deeper in Italy than elsewhere in Europe, making an impress which even free America can hardly efface? Let William Dean Howells, surely a competent and candid observer, respond to this point. "I do not think," he writes in "Venetian Life," "there is ever shown among Italians either the aggressive pride or the abject meanness which marks the intercourse of peoples and nobles elsewhere in Europe; and I have not seen the distinction of rich and poor made so brutally in Italy as sometimes in our own *soi-disant* democratic society at home. There is, indeed, that equality in Italian fibre which I believe fits the nation for democratic institutions better than any other, and which is perhaps partly the result of their ancient civilization."

The same observer in his "Italian Journeys" notes a curious resemblance which may be reassuring to those who are prone to conjure up the bugbear of Italian incapacity for progressive assimilation with Americans and

Americanism. In the head of Pompey he marked the "resemblance to American politicians which I had noted in all the Roman statues." "Pompey," he continued, "was like the picture of so many Southern congressmen."

If it be rejoined gravely that the head of Pompey is not in the scale to-day but the heads of his countrymen nearly two thousand years after he served as a model, perhaps the observation of Gladstone may be more convincing. On the 18th of February, 1861, the first Parliament of United Italy met at Turin. From the very opening of this exacting test was there any lack shown of capacity for good government? On the contrary, for Mr. Gladstone wrote to a correspondent, Sir James Lacaita, at the end of 1862, "My confidence in the Italian Parliament and people increases from day to day. Their self-command, moderation, patience, firmness and forethought reaching far into the future, are really beyond all praise." Apparently this representative infant would bear comparison even with our latest exhibit of Congress.

The innate bent of the Italian for politics is, in truth, strongly marked and nowhere is this more plainly shown than in America, in spite of the common handicaps of unfamiliarity with our language and the absorbing demands of his struggle to earn a living. He is quick to comprehend the use and possible force of his ballot here and is eager to become naturalized as soon as he makes up his mind to make this country his home. This is signally shown in the extraordinary percentage of naturalized Italians in comparison with the total number of Italian birth in New York City. The carefully prepared records of the commission established by the Italian Chamber of Commerce show that 191,289 of the 225,026 persons of Italian parentage living in the city in 1900 were born or naturalized Americans, comprehending 83.4 per cent. of the total Italian population.

The Italian is keen, too, in the study of his advantage in political affiliations and in local, state and national party contests. The more influential soon win their own following and swing organizations with as much dexterity as any other district leaders. There is no device of American politics which they cannot readily master, and they are already a force which no party can afford to neglect in any closely divided district, city or State.

There is nothing surprising in this ready appreciation and adaptability in view of the natural quickness of mind of the Latin races and the correspondence now existing between Italian and American political institutions. Like the American, the present Italian institutions are mainly derived from English models, though the Italian are a closer copy of the English to-day, in spite of their being a French translation. In Italy, as in England and America, "individual liberty, the inviolability of property and of domicile, freedom of the press, of speech and of asso-

Bird's-Eye View of Truck Farming District, near Humboldt, Tennessee.
Cultivated by Thrifty Italian Colonists

ciation, are guaranteed." In the eye of the law "equal rights and liberties are granted to all citizens," says Luigi Villari. Usually the franchise is restricted to the payers of direct taxes, or of farm or house rent, at or over a fixed minimum. The proportion of voters to the total population is stated by Villari to be seven per cent., but this percentage is advancing steadily with the rising ability to read and write, another requirement for the franchise. Even if an Italian has not acquired the right to vote in his own country, he is likely to press for it the more urgently here because his poorest neighbor may now excel him in privilege, power and pride.

A further objection is raised to Italian immigration that its influx is adding to the heterogeneous character of our population and inevitably rendering the problem of assimilation more difficult of solution. It it claimed that the immigration from Northern Europe has been chiefly our kinsfolk, begotten from common stock, whence sprang our Anglo-Saxon institutions, and sharing our aims and ambitions. It is remarked that the assimilation of this stock has naturally been easy and rapid, and that in the second generation there were no hyphenated Americans. "And why not? Because these immigrants were our racial cousins and brothers, taking their places in our national home as naturally as though born under the same roof-tree, since the difference was one in fact, not of birth blood, but of birthplace."

The Italian in America

This happy condition has been gravely disturbed, it is said, by the advent of immigration from Italy and in general from Southern Europe of alien racial stocks "which have not known the ancestral ties and associations and sentiments and trend of the old stock as the earlier immigrants knew and shared them." It is claimed that these differing strains of blood are essentially antagonistic to our own and can only be assimilated with great difficulty and delay, and possibly never.

There is an obvious assumption, to start with, that the gravity of the problem of assimilation advances with the number of the races to be assimilated, and that heterogeneity is in itself a ground of valid objection. It is easier to assert than to maintain this by any convincing proof. It is urged in opposition by close students of the subject, whose examinations are entitled to careful consideration, that heterogeneity under certain conditions, and especially under those existing in America, inevitably operates to advance assimilation instead of retarding it.

"When one race enters the home of another," as one observer remarks, "racial prejudice and racial vanity will cause comparisons that are bitter and dangerous, as they are when two individuals are compared. When there are several races in the field of comparison, ill-feeling cannot be so easily aroused. You may tell Mr. Jones that Mr. Smith is the most intelligent man in the street, and Mr. Jones will show no irritation at this comparison of Mr. Smith with himself and others. But tell Mr. Jones that Mr. Smith is more intelligent than he is and you will straightway observe some symptoms of wounded vanity.

"While there are many races of immigrants to America, they may be greeted with prejudice, but it cannot be as bitterly shown and cannot continue as long as it would if there were only two elements concerned. One race will not continue to strut before all the others, and it is not likely that any two or three will unite in strong prejudice against the rest. When prejudice and bigotry are eliminated, different races will readily associate and assimilation will be rapid.

"As the number of immigrant races has taken the bitterness from prejudice against immigration, so also the establishment of the Jews has done away with the ill-feeling that existed between Catholics and Protestants in America. A religious body will not attack two others with the virulence that it can show toward a single rival, and it would be absurd for two religious elements to quarrel while there is a third in the field to laugh at the contestants. The Jewish immigration has been a blessing for this very reason, and the heterogeneous character of immigration is as great a blessing, since it has relieved us of the danger of racial movements in the United States."

A striking example of undeniable assimilation is the one cited by the editor of the "McKeesport News," November 11, 1903, in his intelligent discussion of "The Immigration Problem."

"Massachusetts, so often called the cradle of liberty and the cornerstone of the American government, now has a population of 2,806,346, one-third of which is foreign born, while considerably more than half of the whole number have foreign-born parents. This large proportion of the foreign element is exceeded by that of only two other states in the Union, and the old Bay State can no longer be looked upon as the exclusive home of the Yankee.

"But nothing proves more conclusively the virility of the native New England stock than the fact that despite this preponderance of foreign born and foreign blood within her borders, Massachusetts still remains distinctively American. The old-time ideas and customs continue, and there has been no change either in the laws or institutions in order to adapt the State to its new inhabitants. The standard of pure Americanism seems to be as securely planted as it ever was. Massachusetts is performing her duty of absorbing the many diverse nationalities which have come under her dominion, and is gradually welding the combined product into a citizenship which is an improvement in some respects over the unemotional remnants of our ancestral race who never came west, but stayed to ossify or decay along the inhospitable and barren interior of old New England.

Progressive Education and Assimilation

" The people who are now taking possession of Massachusetts are Canadian, Irish, English, Swedish, Scotch, German, Russian, Italian, Polish and Portuguese. Ireland has given the greatest number of immigrants, with Canada next in order. Other countries are far in the rear of these two as contributors to the population.

" The success with which Massachusetts has met the immigration problem indicates that we have little to fear from healthy, law-abiding aliens coming from Europe to start life anew in a more promising land. America is so firmly wedded to its customs, language and religious beliefs; its institutions, laws and principles of government are so securely established and are all so liberal, well-directed and beneficent that the foreigner in the course of a few years' residence becomes so thoroughly Americanized that he assists rather than impedes the progress of the country towards its inevitable continental sovereignty and glorious destiny."

These points appear to be well taken, and the view in general is confirmed by the attested rapidity of assimilation in this country and particularly in New York City, where the variety and divergencies of racial types are probably greater than in any city in the world. In an interesting discussion of this subject in his lecture on "The Key to the Twentieth Century," Dr. Thomas Green has characterized the ability of the United States to absorb and Americanize foreign elements as one of the most wonderful achievements of the nation, and the most hopeful sign of its stability. He notes how after a year or two in the public schools the children of foreign birth or descent "come trooping down the steps of the schoolhouse with little flags in their right hands and singing 'My Country, 'Tis of Thee.'" They are just as good Americans in his eye as though their forefathers had been here before the Revolution.

The certainty of this remarkable progress toward assimilation by no means conveys, of course, any license to neglect the precautions assuring Americanization. There are grave exceptions and shortcomings in this progress, particularly in the coal-mining districts, which urgently need attention and remedy. But it is absurd to deny or distrust the assimilating powers of this country because of the scandalous lack in certain localities of proper sanitary and educational provisions as well as of any active sympathy and co-operation with the struggling immigrants.

Rabbi Fleischer has conspicuously punctured the claim, too, that the older immigrants were essentially of the material whereof to make "an Anglo-American alliance." "If the Irish feel somewhat related to the English," he said in a discussion at a meeting in Boston in the winter of 1903-04, "they feel it very disagreeably, and the Jews, so dominant in New York to-day, certainly are not related to the English."

Progressive Education and Assimilation

There is substantial reason for holding that the rapidity of assimilation is more largely dependent on social conditions, the intimacy of distribution, the fusion of classes and the common education and language than upon any approximation of racial strains. Particular encouragement for this view may be drawn from a racial characteristic of the Italian, such as was claimed for the Greek in the famous funeral oration put by Thucidides in the mouth of Pericles. This is a distinguishing faculty of adaptation—Eutrapelos—"a happy and gracious flexibility," as Matthew Arnold translates it. This conforming faculty is not only obvious in the issue of intermarriages, but in the very plain Americanization of the children born in America of native Italian parents. Howells and other observers, too, have particularly noted the readiness with which almost all Italians learn English and their quick appreciation of American progressiveness and in particular of the necessity of the American standard of education for the advancement of their children.

Furthermore, the fear lest the purity of the "Anglo-Saxon strain" be defiled by the alien influx from Southern Europe is only a conceit in grave clothes, which has been too often resurrected. Daniel Defoe flayed it alive two hundred years ago, but its corpse has often been paraded in this country and elsewhere, in spite of its ancient and fishlike smell. When alarmists in England took offence at the entry of the Dutch with William of

The Italian in America

Orange at the English Revolution, Defoe wrote keenly, in spite of the rudeness of his satire, in the "True-Born Englishman":

> "For Englishmen to boast of generation
> Cancels their knowledge and lampoons the nation
> A true-born Englishman's a contradiction,
> In speech an irony, in fact a fiction.
>
>   .   .   .   .
>
> These are the heroes that despise the Dutch,
> And rail at newcome foreigners so much.
> Forgetting that themselves are all derived
> From the most scoundrel race that ever lived;
> A horrid crowd of gambling thieves and drones,
> Who ransacked kingdoms and dispeopled towns;
> The Pict and painted Briton, treacherous Scot,
> Norwegian pirates, buccaneering Danes,
> Whose red-haired offspring everywhere remains;
> Who, joined with Norman French, compound the breed
> From whence your true-born Englishmen proceed."

Moreover, upon what examination worthy of the name has the Southern Latin stock, as exhibited in Italy, for example, been stamped as "undesirable?" Is it undesirable to perpetuate the blood, the memorials and traditions of the greatest empire of antiquity, which spread the light of its civilization from the Mediterranean to the North Sea and the Baltic? Does a stigma recall that this stock was the fountain head of the Renaissance that dispelled the gloom of the Middle Ages? What authority proscribes the land that gave birth to Galileo, the most forceful demonstrator of the earth's motion and orbit, and to Columbus and the Cabots, who brought the New World to light " to redress the balance of the Old? " How strange is this flaunt of prejudice in the faces of Dante and Tasso and Petrarch—of Raphael and Michael Angelo and Canova—of Verdi and Rossini, Bellini and Donizetti—of Ristori and Duse and Salvini and Rossi—of Alfieri and Giacometti—of Cavour, Mazzini and Garibaldi! What freak of conceit ignores historians like Carlo Botta and Pasquale Villari, romancists like Manzoni and D'Annunzio, masters of language like Bartelli and De Amicis, and overlooks astronomers like Schiaparelli and electricians like Ferraris and Marconi, on the loftiest ranges of applied science ? In the field of railway engineering there are no more extraordinary memorials than the three grand passageways of the Mt. Cenis, St. Gothard and Simplon tunnels, the enduring monuments of "Southern Latin " engineers and constructors; and the superb Turin Exposition in its exhibit of the advances of Italian artificers of every kind is an ample rejoinder to any questioning of the capacity of Italian artisans measured by any existing standard of progress.

It may be rejoined that this stamp of disparagement was not·really meant to apply to the Italian artist and artisan, but only to the mass of immigration from the agricultural districts. Is there then any better reason for the proscription of the Italian farm hand, grape grower or market gardener? If their competence as agricultural laborers is in question, there is abundant witness to their efficiency, even under the handicap of primitive tools and methods. A recent observer of unquestioned independence, standing and opportunity for thorough observation, P. D. Fischer, has written to this effect in his able survey "Italien und die Italiener am Schlusse des neunzehnten Jahrhunderts:" "Perhaps the greatest advantage of Italian agriculture lies in the character of the men who practice it. He who has seen with his own eyes the peasant at work will cease talking about Italian indolence. Notwithstanding his ignorance, this peasant is the very best kind of material. If inferior in physical strength to the Swiss, German or English laborer, he is the equal of the representative of any other nation whatever in native intelligence and persistent application to business; while he certainly surpasses them all in thrift, sobriety and good temper." A sufficient reason noted by Herr Fischer for the relative lack of advance and prosperity of the Italian agriculturist is the fundamental and thus far insuperable obstacle of land monopoly in Italy.

Does their poverty unfit them for America? The pitiful meagreness of the living of masses of people in the depressed districts is unquestioned. There is just compassion for the wretched lives of the charcoal burners of the Maremma, for the women toiling on the rice lands of the Romagna from dawn to sunset, for the thousands of weary straw plaiters, sometimes earning no more than twenty centesimi or four cents a day, and for those even more miserable, like the sufferers making dwellings of holes in the rocks at Grotta Rossa, who may be seen at any time beside a spring or rivulet, dipping in the water a handful of leaves or a few fresh bean pods to be eaten as a salad with their dry, hard bread.

One may fail to see, however, anything in this dejection of living that can be brought up as a cause for exclusion in view of the door held open heretofore without any disastrous effect to the poorest peasants of the north of Europe, and especially to the famine-stricken people of Ireland. There is nothing in the condition of any part of Italy more wretched and depressing than was seen in Ireland during the rising tide of immigration to this country. "I remember," writes a German traveller in Ireland at the time of the famine, "when I saw the poor Letts in Livonia, I used to pity them for having to live in huts built of the unhewn logs of trees, the crevices being stopped with moss. . . . Well, Heaven pardon my ignorance! Now that I have seen Ireland, it seems to me that the Letts, the Esthonians and the Finlanders lead a life of comparative comfort, and poor Paddy would feel like a king with their house, their habiliments and their daily fare. . . . A French author, Beaumont, who had seen the Irish peasant in his cabin and the North American Indian in his wigwam, has assured us that the savage is better provided for than the poor man in Ireland. . . .

"A Russian peasant, no doubt, is the slave of a harder master, but still he is fed and housed to his content and no trace of mendicancy is to be seen in him. The Hungarians are certainly not among the best-used people in the world, still what wheat and bread and what wine has even the humblest among them for his daily fare! . . . Servia and Bosnia are reckoned among the most wretched countries of Europe, but, at least, the people, if badly housed, are well clad.

"In Ireland beggary or abject poverty is the prevailing rule. . . . It seems as if wretchedness had prevailed there from time immemorial—as if rags had succeeded rags, bog formed over bog, ruins given birth to ruins and beggars had begotten beggars for a long series of centuries."

Outside of the comparatively small number of political refugees and others driven from their native land by intentional persecution, the masses that have come over from Europe have crossed the ocean intentionally to better their condition and uplift their so-called "standard of living." The existence of lower standards in Europe with scarcely an exception has failed to depress the American standard of living, which has indeed risen progressively in spite of the low standard bugbear. If immigrants were contented they would not have cut all their home ties to come to this country, and there is no ground for assuming that the Italians are backward in lifting themselves to the American standard.

Is their blood of so lowly an extraction that it is likely to impair the fluid that has been transmitted from our Pilgrim forefathers or the first families of Virginia, or the Dutch patroons or other stocks expecting homage? Without pausing to examine the actual mixtures in the veins of our early colonists, which the late Senator Hoar and others have particularly noted, it is probably sufficient to observe that any dread of defilement may be relieved by the assurance of Charles Kingsley: "The physical and intellectual superiority of the high born is only preserved as it was in the old Norman times by the continual practical abnegation of the very caste lie on which they pride themselves, by continual renovation of their race by intermarriage with the ranks below them. The blood of Odin flowed in the veins of Norman William; true—and so did the tanner's of Falaise." Even without the benefit of the infusion of rich old American blood, there appears to be much promise in the offspring of the poorest Italian stocks where the nurturing conditions are even slightly favorable.

In the closing year of our Civil War William Dean Howells examined the work of the "Protestant Ragged Schools" at Naples only a few years after they were "established by the wise philanthropy of the Protestant residents." The foundation of these schools was not older "than the union of Naples with the Kingdom of Italy (in 1860) when toleration of Protestantism was decreed by law."

In spite of the declaration of the Protestant character of the schools and the fact that the Protestant Bible was placed in the hands of the children to be studied and understood, "the parents of the children were so anxious to secure them the benefits of education that they willingly ran the risk of their becoming heretics." These parents were principally "people of the lower classes—laborers, hackmen, fishermen, domestics and very small shop keepers." The first undertaking of the teachers of these schools was to wash the children, educating them "corporeally first of all." Then they set about "cleansing them morally," and next began to educate them in various branches of learning.

The good effects of the training were felt almost immediately. When Mr. Howells visited the schools, he saw that the text-books were kept neat and clean, as were the hands and faces of the children. He attended a regular exercise of the reading class of girls and was strongly impressed by the exceptional average of proficiency. All the girls in the class "seemed to have a lively understanding of what they read,"—and he "never heard American children of their age read nearly so well."

Progressive Education and Assimilation

There was "not a clouded countenance—nor a dirty hand among them." "We should have great hopes for a nation of which the children can be taught to wash themselves." The boys in the upper classes, he reports, were "well up in their studies." Their drawing books were "prodigies of neatness, and betrayed that aptness for form and facility of execution which are natural to the Italian." The feasibility of carrying children of even the most ignorant people in Italy far above the range of elementary education was demonstrated in these schools in the extension of studies to higher mathematics, linear drawing, the French language and courses in Italian and ancient history.

Under the depressing influences of their surroundings and a lack of any stimulus of competition and distinct prospect of advancement, it is not to be wondered at that there was a noticeable flagging in attendance and application after the majority had acquired an elementary education, but the demonstration of their teachableness was incontestable. "Up to a certain point," indeed, as Mr. Howells observes, "the Neapolitan children learn so rapidly and willingly that it can be hardly other than a pleasure to teach them." "Just and consistent usage," he noted further, "has the best influence upon them, and one boy was pointed out as quite docile and manageable whose parents had given him up as incorrigible before he entered the school." He observed too that "the boys of these schools never played truant and are never severely beaten in school."

It was remarkable also that these "heretic schools" excited so little animosity and interference. Only one isolated attempt to hamper the progress of these schools on the part of any of the Neapolitan clergy was noted, and the young scholars had no plaguing to fear from the mass of the street children. This is largely attributable, as Mr. Howells thought, to the "peaceful, uncombative nature of Italian boys, who get on with much less way-laying and thumping and bullying than boys of Northern blood." Whatever the reason, none of them were "molested by their companions who still lived the wild life of the streets."

These observations of Mr. Howells are fully confirmed by the results of my own wide-ranging personal investigations and inquiries. The appreciation of education here appears to be intensified by the limitation or denial of its privileges under the conditions existing in Italy before unification. Even the most ignorant who have come here are quick to see how essential it is to progress, and they are determined that their children shall not be hampered for lack of it like themselves.

"In all grades of the New York City schools," as Mr. Lawrence Franklin has noted, "teachers agree in commending the intelligence and studiousness of Italian children, for next to the Jews they are the best scholars in the matter of application. The boys are especially clever in drawing, modelling and manual work which requires delicate fingers. The girls are better in languages and history. One has only to pay a visit to the Baxter Street school and observe the number of neat, bright looking Italian children there to realize how unjust we have been in treating this race as outcasts and aliens."

Jacob A. Riis attests the same teachableness of the Italian children and the effect of their education extending to their homes and parents. After remarking the original doubts or prejudice of their instructors here, he notes the disappearance of their distrust and how "today the Italian children are gladly welcomed. Their sunny temper, which no hovel is dreary enough, no hardship has power to cloud, has made them universal favorites, and the discovery has been made by their teachers that, as the crowds pressed harder, their school rooms have marvelously expanded, until they embraced within their walls an unsuspected multitude, even many a slum tenement itself, cellar, stoop, attic and all. Every lesson of cleanliness, of order, and of English taught at the school is reflected into some wretched home and rehearsed there as far as the limited opportunity will allow."

The assimilating effect of contact and education here is also particularly remarked by Dr. J. H. Senner, for many years Commissioner of Immigration at the port of New York. "The common opinion," he writes, "as to the inability of Italian immigrants to assimilate, is, I am frank to state, not shared by me. The acquirement of English is no more difficult to mature Italians than to other non-English speaking immigrants; children born in this country of Italian parents can scarcely be distinguished by their speech or their habits from the children of native Americans. The public schools of New York bear testimony to this statement. The Rev. Bonaventure Piscopo, of the Church of the Most Precious Blood (the largest Italian Roman Catholic Parish in the United States), is my authority for the statement that all the Italian priests, in their religious services, their Sunday school and even in their confessionals, are obliged to use the English if they hope to be understood at all by the second generation."

The expert observation of Jacob Riis further assures the certainty of assimilation and progress even under the most unfavorable conditions. Of the advance of the Neapolitan immigrant he says: "Starting thus, below the bottom as it were (in the congested heart of New York City), he has an uphill journey before him to work out of the slums, and the promise, to put it mildly, is not good. He does it all the same, or if not he, his boy. It is not an Italian sediment that breeds the tough. Parental authority has a strong enough grip on the lad in Mulberry Street to make him work and that is his salvation. 'In seventeen years,' said the teacher of the oldest Italian

ragged school in the city, that day and night takes in quite
six hundred, 'I have seen my boys work up into decent
mechanics and useful citizens almost to a man, and of my
girls only two I know of have gone astray.' I have observed the process often enough myself to know that she
was right. It is to be remembered, furthermore, that her
school is in the very heart of the Five Points district, and
takes in always the worst and the dirtiest crowd of children.''

This expert evidence of the teachableness of the children
is confirmed by hundred of reports which I obtained from
teachers and others in intimate contact with the Italian
children in all American States where Italians are now
living in considerable numbers. It is impracticable to
do more than summarize this mass of testimony here, but
a sample report received from Mr. L. H. Lancaster, Secretary of the Lafourche Progressive Union, Thibodaux,
Louisiana, is quoted in part, as the Italian immigration
to Louisiana has been mainly of the class that has been
accounted most ignorant and unprogressive.

"The class with which I have come in contact," writes
Mr. Lancaster, "is not what would be considered desirable, being entirely of the Sicilian type. While the original infusion was of a low class, illiterate and tending to
be unruly and used only for hard manual labor, having
had no training nor education and not being adaptable
for scientific pursuits nor for diversified or intensified agri-

cultural pursuits without close attention—yet I can say
that their offspring are the brightest and most ambitious
and quickest of perception that we have in the public
schools. Moreover, they are of a very amiable and polite
disposition.''

From hundreds of available instances also of exceptional proficiency, I may quote one recorded in the "Rochester (N. Y.) Times" of July 6, 1904, as follows:

"That the immigration danger is not the bugaboo that
many folks are inclined to consider it is evidenced in the
fact that two of the five free scholarships in the Department of Mechanic Arts at the Mechanics Institute this
year go to foreign youths, one a Russian-German who
was unable to speak English four years ago when he arrived in this country, and the other, the son of an Italian
laborer. These scholarships entitle the holder to three
years' instruction in a mechanical, architectural or engineering course and are worth $225 each. They were
won in brisk competition, the examinations dealing with
the subjects, arithmetic, geography, grammar and American history.

"Israel Bernhardt and Dominic Lucca give promise of
being successful men and a credit to their race as well as
to the proud country of their adoption."

Kate Holliday Claghorn, Assistant Registrar of Records of the "Tenement House Department" of New
York City, further meets the point of complaint which

has been brought against Italian parents with seeming injustice. "The Italians have been reproached," she writes, "with denying advantages to their children for the sake of the money to be got by the children's labor, but a special investigation, made some years ago by a committee of sociological specialists, shows that the charge, when made a general one, is without foundation. The committee testified in the plainest terms to the fact that the Italian family, even in circumstances of the greatest destitution, showed at least the normal amount of interest in the education of their children, and in many cases made special sacrifices to secure it."

As a matter of course, assimilation is slower in the case of the adult immigrant than in that of his children, but there is no reason to question a more or less steady and hopeful progress of the mass of the immigrants, both women and men, in proportion to their opportunities for advance and the years of their settlement. Their education by contact and observation goes on irresistibly, and the extent of their enlightenment through newspapers and books is not ordinarily realized.

Italians who can read are commonly fond of reading and those who have not learned to read will listen eagerly to any reading they can understand. The number and circulation of the Italian newspapers in this country show the rising appreciation of the news of the day on the part of the newcomers unable as yet to read the papers printed

in English. Yet the stated number of copies printed by
any Italian publisher is far below the actual circulation,
for the copies pass from hand to hand and reach a number of readers far in excess of the subscribers or buyers.
The practice of reading aloud from a paper to a circle of
acquaintances eager to hear the news or miscellany or
editorial appeals or advertisements vastly expands also
the nominal range of these mediums.

The recent inquiry of a reporter for the New York "Sun"
brought out also very clearly the extent of another practice, the borrowing of books which the readers are too
poor to buy. One book peddlar told the reporter that
for the first privilege of reading an uncut book he charged
about a third of the market price. "The next half dozen
readers paid about 20 cents on the dollar. Finally it ran
down by stages as low as 10 cents or even 5 for a week's
use, and then the boys on the ferry boats and the like get
their turn at it.

"'And where do you get your books,' the walking
library was asked.

"'At the banker's,' was the reply.

"Nobody can tell just why all the Italian booksellers
in New York except the newspaper publishers are bankers, but they are. Not all the Italian bankers are booksellers, but every bookseller is a banker.

"There are from a dozen to twenty of them, at least
one or two in each Italian center, and some of them do

a very large trade. Many thousands of volumes are imported by them every year, chiefly from Milan, Florence and Rome, and besides their local sales one or two of them send out consignments of books to other parts of the country where there are large Italian settlements.

"Some idea of the extent of the Italian book trade in New York may be formed from the fact that one banker-bookseller, one of the largest, publishes a copiously illustrated book catalogue of 176 pages, with a fancy cover representing the United States as a handsome female figure all spangled over with stars, twining one arm about a pretty Italian woman with a child, while with the other hand she points to the setting sun, against which the Statue of Liberty and an ocean steamship are silhouetted.

"The books embraced in the catalogue cover the whole educational field to begin with. Books for the study of English and Italian are numerous; dictionaries and grammars take up more than a page. Works of religious instruction, Italian and general history are well covered. The decorative arts and sciences, abstract and applied, fill many pages."

The representative heads of the cities chiefly attracting Italian immigration and settlement are among the most positive in their conviction of the feasibility of assimilation, and their attestation of the industry, thrift, good conduct and certain advance to good citizenship of the mass of the Italian immigrants. In general accord with this view too are the most active members of the Board of Education, city school teachers, public and private, and the clergy coming most closely in contact with the immigrants and their children.

The present Mayor of New York, George B. McClellan, has been particularly observant of the Italian character and progress, even under conditions must unfavorable to hopeful development, and has repeatedly emphasized his belief in their certain advance to good citizenship. In a notably incisive discussion of the relation of education to immigration, reported by Mr. James Creelman in "The New York World," May 22nd, 1904, the Mayor summed up his view pithily in closing.

"Already we are beginning to feel the good effect of our schools upon our foreign-born population. Take the Italians, for instance. They are being assimilated very swiftly. The number of them who take out citizenship papers increases every year. They make good citizens. So I find with other nationalities. The schools are gradually turning all the elements that come to this great clearing port of the American Continent into a common and admirable civic type—American to the core."

ELIOT LORD.

CHAPTER XII

A common objection has been raised to the entry of the mass of Italian immigration to this country, on the score that it has been too largely attracted by the narrow consideration of money-making and not with any purpose of identifying the Italian with American home interests and citizenship. In other words, the mass of immigrants have been reputed to be so-called "birds of passage," coming here for the sake of the high wages of the American labor market, and scrimping their standard of living in order to accumulate savings sufficient to enable them to return home and lift themselves above the level of their former condition.

There is an offset, not always recognized, to this objection in the fact that the supply of labor thus obtained is flexible, adjusting itself readily to the demands of the labor market. Hence the pressure in times of depression is relieved more easily than in cases where the immigrants have established homes which they can hardly leave without costly sacrifices, if at all. So in times of great industrial activity labor flows in like the advance of the tide, receding as naturally with the falling off of the demand in periods of stagnation or industrial collapse.

So far, therefore, as the influx is viewed in strict relation to its effects on the labor market, it may be conceded that the freedom from attachment of immigrant labor is of material value in its elastic response to the operation of the laws of supply and demand. The relief afforded to the American workman by the return of laborers across the ocean in times of stringency is greater than could have been effected if their settlement had been more stable.

Nevertheless I have no desire to minimize the force of the objection to any influence that tends to retard assimilation and impairs the identification of workingmen here with American interests and citizenship. Any temporary relief from the strain of competition would be too dearly secured if the permanent national welfare of the country was sacrificed. It is unquestionably to the interest of this country that the mass of its working population shall be moved by higher considerations than the bare pecuniary incentive which temporary employment affords.

We want American workingmen generally to look upon this country as their country, to realize their identification with its free institutions, its aims and its future, and to be intimately fused in association as fellow American citizens, and not to be held aloof as sojourners and aliens.

It does not appear, however, that any novel restrictions

are necessary to effect this assimilation. The flow and return of labor will doubtless proceed in years to come as in the past, but there is no reason to apprehend any increase in its percentage in comparison with the volume of population. The actual amount of this floating labor has never exceeded one per cent. of our population, a number relatively inconsiderable in view of the vast majority that have taken and will continue to take a permanent residence and part in the advance of our republic.

If there is any force in the reproach that the Italians in particular have looked upon this country as a place for money-making rather than as a home, the edge of this reproach is becoming more blunt year after year with the changing views of the immigrants and the rising appreciation of the opportunities open to the Italian in America and the reasons why he should prize a home and citizenship here. The percentage of Italian women, mothers, wives and daughters coming to this country has been steadily increasing with the rising number of immigrants bringing their families with them or calling them over as soon as the men have secured homes to receive them. Thus far the marriages of Italian women have been almost wholly with the men of their own nationality or descent, but a large percentage of the men have intermarried with other nationalities, and this percentage is further expanded by the marriage of the American-born sons of the immigrants.

The Italian in America

The advancing attachment to America is further marked, too, by the greater stability of settlement and acquisition of property. Even the city tenement quarters now occupied by Italians are largely passing into the hands of Italian owners, as has been before noted, and the progress of naturalization is extending throughout the country with the advance of permanent settlement. It would appear to be no longer necessary to urge upon the Italian residents of New York City, for example, the advantages of naturalization, for a recent examination has shown that 111,696 out of a total of 145,433 of persons born in Italy of Italian parentage were naturalized in 1900. The percentage of applicants for citizenship is naturally not so large in the newer and more infirm settlements, but there nowhere appears any reason to question that Italians as a body seek citizenship as zealously as the immigrants of any other nationality. They are quick to see that it places them on an equal footing of rights and privileges with the native American or naturalized associate of any nationality. It is the stamp that marks their entire and loyal identification with the American people in the maintenance and advance of a republic in which all citizens are fellow partners. It gives them a representative voice in the framing of the laws that govern and in the choice of their magistrates. It assures to them the respect that is accorded inevitably to fellow citizens and qualified voters. It opens to them the offices in the gift of American citizens or of the men of their election, by ballot, appointment, or civil service examination. It gives access to any reservations of employment or privilege for the exclusive benefit of American citizens.

It serves to break down irresistibly the lingering bars of aversion or distrust or indifference that separate the alien from the citizen. They see in it, too, a bulwark of protection against any imposition and a certificate of power to compel the fair recognition that rival political parties must give to the foreign-born citizens of any nationality in this country when the determination of political control may be dependent upon their votes.

In short, the privileges and advantages of American citizenship are so material and so manifest that the Italian-American will indeed be dull-witted if he does not seek to acquire them when the opportunity is offered. It is, however, of prime importance to him and to his adopted country that he should appreciate its duties no less fully than its opportunities. No Italian has the right legally or morally to apply for American citizenship unless he comprehends to the letter the oath that he takes and is absolutely resolved to be faithful to that oath without a moment of wavering or repining. The American republic asks no applicant for citizenship to forget his fatherland or any of its inspiring memories. It seeks rather to draw the bonds more closely that serve to unite all nations in international fellowship and untroubled peace.

The Italian in America

But the Italian, who has not finally made up his mind, whatever natural regrets he may cherish, to sever his former allegiance and transfer to his adopted country the full measure of loyalty and duty that was due to his native land, is not qualified for admission to American citizenship. If home still means to him his dear birthplace and he still hopes to return not simply as a welcome visitor, but as an adventurer who has filled his pockets with American gold, he is not entitled to the citizenship which he has sought only as a means to this end.

If, on the contrary, with all due reverence for his original fealty, he surrenders it with a true heart to take up the new loyalty and obligations imposed by his shift of citizenship, he will be truly welcome to American fellowship.

Henceforth the Stars and Stripes will be his flag as surely as it is the flag of any native-born citizen, and he must follow it, whether he be rich or poor, to the death, if need be, when he is called upon by his adopted country to prove his fidelity.

Before he applies for citizenship, the Italian who comes to this country must take to heart, too, that American citizenship is a trust that he must hold sacred—that its duties and responsibilities are confided to his honor—that he must shrink from any proposal to prostitute it as he would from a known lure of the devil in any guise. There will be traps set for his feet as soon as he has won the right to vote and before—offers to pay the fee for citizenship papers and other inducements for the promise of his support at the polls—bids for his vote on Election Day by unscrupulous partisans—or the more covert and dangerous appeals to his prejudice or personal favoritism. The temptations thus set in the way of a poor man are too often triumphant. They should brand with shame the face of the tempters, but the tempted cannot take the stain off their honor by any excuse for yielding to shameful inducements. All who sell their votes under any pretence violate their oath of citizenship, break the law against such venality, make themselves liable to arrest, trial, conviction and imprisonment, and disgrace not only themselves but the nationality which is obliged to own them as fellow countrymen. There has unfortunately been ground for the charge that some Italian-Americans have taken their oath of allegiance too lightly and have been willing to sell or barter their votes as if they were trinkets on which they set little value. It should be needless to point out that this reckless and shameful abuse of citizenship must be rooted out by every means at the command of good citizenship as a foul blot on the face of our republic and a cancer that may eat to the heart of the integrity of republican institutions.

It is the duty of all Italian-American citizens and applicants for citizenship to inform themselves in every feasible way in regard to the questions of public concern whose settlement may be affected by their influence or votes.

If they cannot read or understand English readily, they may study the presentation of these questions in Italian-American journals, and may call on their own best informed countrymen in America or others upon whose honesty and fairness they can rely for the needed explanation. Every meeting for such discussion is helpful if sincerely conducted. No one should be content with biased or one-sided presentations. Let both sides have an impartial hearing and let the statements and evidence submitted by both be carefully and fairly considered. Let the decision in every case be in accordance with every man's conviction of duty to himself, his family and his country. Then, even if mistaken, the determination will be right and one of which no citizen need be ashamed.

It is the duty further of every applicant for citizenship to exalt the standard of American citizenship in his personal conduct and by every influence at his command. He should be sober, truthful, honest, law-abiding, industrious, thrifty and ambitious for the advance of himself and his children. He should prize the free thought, free press, free school and free government of America as a treasure beyond price. He should learn to rely with confidence on American laws, juries and judges for justice and indemnity for wrongs and not to seek redress by lawless violence. He should never forget that prejudice can most surely be confounded by conduct that may defy the barbs of slander, and that any falling off from this standard of duty will lower not only himself but the reputation of his fellow countrymen in the esteem of America. Let it be his pride to keep ever at heart "I was an Italian. I am an American. I am not conscious that I have done anything to sully the honor of either name."

JOHN J. D. TRENOR.

INDEX

A

Agriculture, Italian, 30-32, 41-48; 233, 234; Italian in America, 88-92, 112-153, 170-174.

Aiken, Hon. Wyatt, advocates better distribution of immigration, 156, 157.

Alabama, Italians in, 6; agricultural development and settlement of, by Italians, 132-134.

Alderson, Indian Territory, Italian miners in, 108.

"American Journal of Sociology," on comparative criminality, 204.

" Americans in Process," sociological publication, 73, 202.

Archibald, Indian Territory, Italian miners in, 108.

Arizona, Italians in, 6.

Arkansas, Italians in, 6; on plantations, 148-153.

" Associated Charities " of Boston, 23d Annual Report of, 195-197.

Asti, Cal., prosperous Italian colony of, 135-142.

B

Baltimore, Italians in, 9.

Belgium, population of in proportion to area, 155.

Boston, Italians in, 8; improvement of Italian lodgings, 73; report of " Associated Charities " of, 195-197; condition of Italians in, 201-203; comparative temperance of Italians in, 214.

Bridgeport, Conn., Italian settlement in, 84, 85.

Brindisi, Rocco, M.D., on comparative diseases and mortality, 199-201, 203.

Bryan, Texas, Italian settlement in, 89, 90.

Buck, C. L., reports on " Italian Labor in the South," 172-174.

Buckingham, City Clerk of Bridgeport, reports on Italian citizenship, 84.

C

California, Italian-born population of, 6; cities of, condition of Italians in, 90-92; attracts immigration, 115; Italian agricultural settlements in, 135-144.

" California Fruit Growers Association," 91.

Canada, Dominion of, promotes immigration, 163-166, 188; assimilation of immigrants from, 228, 229.

Index

Index

England and Wales, proportion of immigrants from, in charitable institutions of New York City, 194, 195; comparative temperance of immigrants from, 212.

F

Fassino Brothers, progressive Italian operators, 108.

Fischer, P. D., on Italian agriculturists, 234.

Fleischer, Rabbi, on racial divergence, 230.

Florida, Italians in, 5.

Fobes, Alan C., Mayor of Syracuse, reports on Italian labor and character, 85.

Fontana, Signor Marco, J., superintendent California Fruit-Growers' Association, 91.

"Four States Immigration League," 183, 184.

Franklin, Lawrence, on Italian teachableness, 240, 241.

French Canada, percentage of unskilled labor furnished by, 65; assimilation of immigrants from, 228, 229.

G

Georgia, Italians in, 5.

Germany, proportion of immigrants from charitable institutions of New York City, 194-195; comparative temperance of immigrants from, 212.

Gladstone, William E., on Italian capacity, 223.

Gordon, F. B., President of Georgia Industrial Association, address of, 116, 117.

Green, Dr. Thomas, "Key to the Twentieth Century," 229-230.

Greenville, Miss., Italian farms and plantations at, 146.

H

Hale, Edward Everett, discusses immigration, 163; appeals for distribution, 181-182.

Harris, U. S. Commercial Agent, report of, 36.

Hart, Hastings H., on comparative criminality of foreign and native-born population, 204, 205.

Hartford, Conn., Italians in, 9.

Hartshorne, Indian Territory, Italian miners in, 108.

Heingartner, Alexander, U. S. Consul at Catania, report of, 47.

Hoboken, N. J., Italians in, 9.

Holyoke, George Jacob, remarks on apathy of American government touching direction of immigration, 181.

Howells, William Dean, on Italian democracy, 222, 223; on "Ragged Schools" of Naples, 237-240.

Hungary, percentage of unskilled labor furnished by, 65.

I

Idaho, Italians in, 6.

Index

Illinois, Bureau of Labor Statistics, report of, 100-102.

Illinois, Italians in, 5.

"Immigrant Fund," 180.

Immigration, of Italians to United States, 1-18; to United States from Italy discussed by Dr. J. H. Senner, 10; report of U. S. Commissioner General of Immigration for year ending June 30, 1903, 12; report of Commissioner for the State of New York, 12; discussed by Inspector of Royal Emigration Department of Italy, 13, 14; restriction of considered in Report of Industrial Commission, 14; comparative ratio of increase of, 15; "educational test" for, 16, 17; objections to, 18; causes and regulation of, from Italy, 36-60; into the coal mining fields, 99-113; into the agricultural districts, 114-154; rising demand for Italian, 155-175; need of better distribution of, 176-189.

Immigration Restriction League, advocates "educational test," 16; reports on criminal record of Italians, 212.

Independence, La., Italian settlement and strawberry culture in, 127-129.

Indiana, Italians in, 5.

Indian Territory, Italians in, 6, 88, 107-110.

Industrial Commission, on Immigration, calculates percentages of immigration from Italy by sexes, 11, 12; considers restriction, 14; records percentage of males employed in principal industries, 64, 65; reports advance of Italians as makers of clothing, 95, 96; gives percentages of pauperism for nationalities, 197; presents comparative criminality, 205.

Iowa, Italians in, 6.

Ireland, percentage of unskilled labor furnished by, 65; depressed condition of during famine, 235, 236.

Irish, percentage residing in American cities, 8; association with Italians, 69, 70; in mining fields, 106, 107; percentage of pauperism, 193, 197; in charitable institutions of the United States, 198; intemperance of, 212; in Massachusetts, 229; relation to English, 230.

Italian, influx of immigration to the United States, 1-4; population in the United States, 5, 9; population in American cities, 8, 9; population in the State of New York, 10; population in Greater New York, 10; immigration with distinction of sex, 10-12; immigration with distinction of ages, 12; immigration, per capita value of, 12, 13; immigration, desirability of, 12-17; immigration, ob-

Index

jections to, 17, 18; inheritance and progress, 20-38; emigration, causes and regulation of, 39-60; settlement in American cities, 61-92; skilled and unskilled labor, 61-66; occupations in cities, 65-68; characteristics, 68; relations with Irish, 69, 70; congestion in cities, 70-73; tenancy and ownership increase property values, 73-78; savings and investments in New York City, 78, 79; business enterprises and charitable foundations, 80, 81; devotion to the fine arts, 81; comparative advance in smaller cities, 81-92; in competition and association, 93-98; in the mining fields, 99-113; on farm and plantation, 116-153; pauperism, disease and crime, 190-220; progressive education and assimilation, 221-248; advance to American citizenship, 249-257.

"Italian Benevolent Institute," 81.

Italy, emigration from, to the United States, 1-18; inheritance and progress of, 20-38; population of, 40; industrial condition of, 40-48.

J

Jersey City, N. J., Italians in, 8.
Jew, the, in competition with Italian clothing worker, 95; in charitable institutions in the United States, 198; establishment of, in United States, 227; not related to English, 230; in public schools, 240.

K

Kansas City, Mo., Italians in, 9.
Kansas, Italians in, 6.
Keller, Hon. John W., reports on pauperism in New York City, 193-195.
Kentucky, Italians in, 6.
Krebs, Indian Territory, Italian miners in, 108-110.

L

La Colonia Alessandrina di Memphis, 124.
La Societa di Muttuo Soccorso dei Giardinieri Italiani di Memphis, 124.
La Tribuna Italiana, 118.
Lamberth, Ala., Italian settlement in, 132, 134.
Lancaster, L. H., on education of Italian children, 243, 244.
Landis, Charles, promotes Italian colonization, 131.
Landisville, N. J., Italian settlement in, 131.
Langley, Lee J., reports on Italians in the South, 174.
Lithuanians, in the mining fields, 103-106.
Lloyd, Henry Demarest, reports on New Zealand's distribution of labor, 177-179.

263

Index

Louisiana, Italians in, 6; condition and character of, 87, 88; Italians in agricultural districts of, 127-129, 144, 145, 152, 172-174, 243, 244.

M

Mabie, Hamilton, notes influence of Italy on Europe, 26.

Madera, Cal., Italian colony at, 142, 143.

Maine, Italians in, 5.

Maryland, Italians in, 5.

Massachusetts, Italians in, 5, 8, 73, 195-197; condition of Italians in, 201, 203; criminal record of Italians in, 212, 213.

Mastro-Valerio, Alessandro, editor and founder of colonies, 118, 119, 131-134.

McAdoo, Police Commissioner, on organization of "Italian Department," 219, 220.

McAlister, Indian Territory, Italian miners in, 108, 109.

McClellan, Geo. B., view of Italian immigration, 248.

McConnell, W. W. P., Dairy and Food Commissioner for Minnesota, report of, 167, 168.

McKeesport "News," "The Immigration Problem," 227-229.

Memphis, Tenn., Italian suburban settlement, 124; application for labor from, 185, 186.

Michigan, Italians in, 5.

Miners, Italian immigrant, 99, 100; number Italian, in anthracite region, 103; Lithuanian, Slovak and Polish, 103; perils of, 104; jealousy and dissensions of, 105; improved condition of, 106; number of Italian, in Indian Territory, 108; satisfactory condition of, in Indian Territory and Texas, 108-112; in Colorado, 113.

Minnesota, Italians in, 6; need of further development, 166-168.

Mississippi, Italians in, 6; on sugar cane plantations, 144-154; Italian labor in, 174.

Missouri, Italians in, 6.

Mitchell, John, President United Mine Workers, opposes immigration, 159-160.

Montana, Italians in, 6.

Mulvihill, Mayor of Bridgeport, reports on Italian character, 84.

N

Naturalization, of Italians, 224, 252, 253.

Nebraska, Italians in, 6.

Nevada, Italians in, 6.

Newark, N. J., Italians in, 8.

New Hampshire, Italians in, 5.

New Haven, Conn. Italians in, 8, 121-123.

New Jersey, Italians in, 5.

New Mexico, Italians in, 6.

New Orleans, Italian settlement in, 87, 88.

New York City, Italian-born population of, 8; Italian settlement in, 69-72, 74-81, 120.

Index

New York "Evening Post," discusses Italian settlement in American cities, 114, 115.

New York State, Italians in, 5; condition of, 85-87; Italian market-gardening in, 124-127.

New York State Board of Charities, report on pauperism, 193-195.

New York "Sun" on emigration to Canada, 165, 166; on emigration to the South, 168; on Italian book readers, 246-248.

New York "Times," reports statement of John Mitchell, 159, 160.

New York "World" reports Mayor Geo. B. McClellan, 248.

New Zealand, Department of Labor, 177-179.

"North American Review," article on "Immigration from Italy," 11.

North Carolina, Italians in, 5.

North Dakota, Italians in, 6.

O

Ohio, Italians in, 5.

Oklahoma, Italians in, 6.

Olino, Dr. G., promoter of viticulture, 138.

Oregon, Italians in, 6.

P

Pantaleone, Prof., on taxation in Italy, 41, 42.

Paterson, Italians in, 8,

Pauperism, in Italy, 191; in New York City, 192-195; in Boston, 195-197; general distribution of, by nationalities in the United States, 197, 198.

Percy, Leroy, planter, 148; reports on Italian labor, 150, 151.

Petrosini, Police Sergeant, heads "Italian Department," 219.

Philadelphia, Italians in, 8.

"Philadelphia Record" discusses immigration, 158, 159.

Philips, Indian Territory, Italian miners in, 108.

Piedmont, miners from, 108-110.

Pittsburg, Italians in, 8.

Pole, the, in competition with Italian clothing-maker, 96; in the mining fields, 103.

Population, Italian, born in the United States, 5; percentage of Italian born in American cities, 8, 9; computed total of Italian descent in the United States, 9; percentage of Russian born in American cities, 10; percentage of Irish born in American cities, 10; total of Italian descent in New York State, 10; in Greater New York, 10.

Preston, W. T. R., Canadian Commissioner, reports on emigration to Canada, 165, 166.

Providence, R. I., Italians in, 8.

R

Raleigh (N. C.) "Observer," on "Italian Immigration to the South," 170-174.

Index

Reich, Emil, discusses "The Future of the Latin Races," 37, 38.

Rhode Island, Italians in, 5.

Riis, Jacob, sets forth evils of congestion, 72; on beggary in New York City, 192, 193; on eradication of the slum, 206-209; teachableness of Italian children, 241; assimilation and progress of Italian immigrants, 242, 243.

Rochester, N. Y., Italians in, 9.

Rochester (N. Y.) "Times," on Italian and Russian competition, 244.

Rossi, Adolpho, Inspector of Royal Emigration Department of Italy, discusses character of Italian emigration to America, 13, 14; notes increase of wages in Italy, 45, 46; presents main provisions of Italian official regulation of emigration, 56-60; reports on Italian settlement in New Orleans, 87, 88; in Bryan and other towns in Texas, 89, 90; in Salt Lake City, 90; in San Francisco and other cities in California, 90-92; reports on Italian miners in Indian Territory, Texas and Colorado, 107-113; inspects settlements in Tennessee, 124; in Louisiana, 128, 129; in California, 140-143; in Texas, 145, 146; in Mississippi, 146, 147; in Arkansas, 148, 149.

Rossi, Pietro C., distinguished

pharmacist, and member of Italian-Swiss Association, 141.

Royal Emigration Department of Italy, organization of, 54, 55; policy of, 56-60.

Russia, percentage of population Russian-born in American cities, 8.

Russian-Poland, percentage of population in American cities, 8.

S

Sacred Heart, missionary sisters of, 80, 88.

San Francisco, Italian-born population of, 8; Italian settlement in, 91, 92.

San Jose, California, Italian settlement in, 92.

"Saturday Review," London, on independence of United States, 189.

St. Joseph Protective Association, 219.

St. Louis, Mo., Italians in, 9.

Sbarboro, Cav. A., a founder of Asti, Cal., 141.

Schenectady, N. Y., Italian settlement in, 85.

Scranton, Pa., Italians in, 9.

Senner, Dr. J. H., discusses "Immigration from Italy," 10, 11; on assimilation of Italian immigrants, 241, 242.

Sex, division of, in Italian immigration to the United States, 10-12.

Index